National Foundation for
Educational Research

Teacher's Handbook

Oxford Reading Tree *Stages 3–5*
Book Bands *Yellow – Green*

Written by

Kate Ruttle

OXFORD
UNIVERSITY PRESS

OXFORD
UNIVERSITY PRESS

is a department of the University of Oxford.
It furthers the University's objective of excellence in research, scholarship,
and education by publishing worldwide in

Oxford   New York

Auckland   Cape Town   Dar es Salaam   Hong Kong   Karachi
Kuala Lumpur   Madrid   Melbourne   Mexico City   Nairobi
New Delhi   Shanghai   Taipei   Toronto

With offices in

Argentina   Austria   Brazil   Chile   Czech Republic   France   Greece
Guatemala   Hungary   Italy   Japan   Poland   Portugal   Singapore
South Korea   Switzerland   Thailand   Turkey   Ukraine   Vietnam

Oxford is a registered trade mark of Oxford University Press
in the UK and in certain other countries

© Oxford University Press 2009

The moral rights of the author have been asserted

Database right Oxford University Press (maker)

First published 2009

Written by Kate Ruttle

Phonics adviser Clare Kirtley
Scotland adviser Louise Ballantyne
Northern Ireland adviser Marion Bailie
Wales adviser Jacqueline Harrett

Oxford Reading Tree is based on the original characters
created by Roderick Hunt and Alex Brychta

All rights reserved. No part of this publication may be reproduced,
stored in a retrieval system, or transmitted, in any form or by any means,
without the prior permission in writing of Oxford University Press,
or as expressly permitted by law, or under terms agreed with the appropriate
reprographics rights organization. Enquiries concerning reproduction
outside the scope of the above should be sent to the Rights Department,
Oxford University Press, at the address above

You must not circulate this book in any other binding or cover
and you must impose this same condition on any acquirer

British Library Cataloguing in Publication Data

Data available

ISBN: 978-0-19-918050-9

10 9 8 7 6 5 4 3 2

Cover photo by Istock/Cat London

Inside illustrations by Alex Brychta,
Chris Mould, Daniel Postgate
and Melanie Williamson

Crown copyright material is reproduced under the terms of the Click-Use Licence

Page make-up by PDQ Digital Media Solutions

Oxford University Press would like to thank all the advisers, reviewers and
trialling schools involved in the development of Oxford Reading Tree
Assess & Progress. We would also like to thank the staff and pupils of
Great Heath Primary School in Mildenhall for allowing us to film them.

Printed in China by Imago

Paper used in the production of this book is a natural, recyclable product
made from wood grown in sustainable forests. The manufacturing process
conforms to the environmental regulations of the country of origin.

Contents

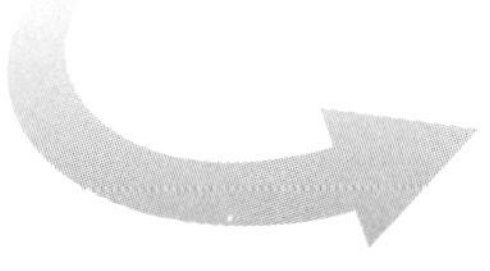

About *Assess & Progress*

Welcome to Oxford Reading Tree *Assess & Progress*.

Assess & Progress provides:

- all the resources you need to make reliable assessments of your children's reading attainment
- diagnostic support to identify possible barriers to reading progress
- ideas and activities to help children develop skills and move forward.

This resource has been developed by the leaders in reading and assessment, Oxford Primary and NFER (National Foundation for Educational Research), to help you assess your children's reading and integrate your findings easily into classroom practice.

NFER and *Assess & Progress*

The National Foundation for Educational Research (NFER) is the UK's leading educational research institution. They work to equip teachers with the most practical research and responsive assessment programmes, assisting with the drive towards excellence in education.

As part of the development of Oxford Reading Tree *Assess & Progress*, NFER researchers:

- independently developed the four-step Reading Assessment for every Benchmark Book
- trialled the Reading Assessments in schools, and verified the results
- selected examples of real-life Reading Assessments for teachers and teaching assistants to use to guide their own practice.

Oxford Reading Tree and *Assess & Progress*

Oxford Reading Tree books, with their proven appeal to children, variety of content and clearly structured progression, represent an ideal foundation for sound assessment practice in the classroom.

The benchmark books in *Assess & Progress* reflect the spread and flexibility of Oxford Reading Tree, and include *Biff, Chip and Kipper* stories, *Songbirds Phonics*, *Snapdragons* variety fiction and *Fireflies* non-fiction.

In developing *Assess & Progress*, NFER and Oxford Reading Tree shared the aim of creating an assessment toolkit that was practical and effective for teachers, and motivating for children.

What is *Assess & Progress?*

Assess & Progress supports your professional judgement in assessing children's reading. It is designed to be easy to integrate into your existing classroom practice, helping you gather useful evidence to demonstrate children's progress in reading. It also provides practical next steps for teaching and learning.

The box contains:

- **Benchmark Books** for Stages 1–11 (Book Bands Pink–Lime), clearly matched to curriculum levels
- a photocopiable four-step **Reading Assessment** for every Benchmark Book, including miscue analysis and comprehension questions
- an **Unseen Text** card for each Stage 1+ to 11, to help you find out more about a child's reading
- **practical teaching support** including photocopiable record and reward sheets, diagnostic support, and next steps advice and activities
- **software** containing a how-to guide, real-life examples of Reading Assessments, editable versions of assessment, record and reward sheets, and Oxford Reading Tree *Assess & Progress* clipart.

When to use *Assess & Progress*

You can use *Assess & Progress* to:

- confirm a reading level for a child who is making progress in reading
- determine whether a child is ready to read books at the next level
- plan for progress in reading for guided or group reading sessions
- set short-, medium- and long-term targets for reading.

How to use this handbook

The *Assess & Progress* Teacher's Handbooks provide you with practical assessment, diagnostic and next steps support.

This handbook has five main sections:

Introduction – pages 4 to 23

This section outlines the structure and key features of Oxford Reading Tree *Assess & Progress*, explaining how it fits with curriculum requirements, assessment and classroom practice in England, Wales, Scotland and Northern Ireland.

How to use *Assess & Progress* – pages 24 to 37

This is a practical guide to using the main assessment resources. It covers the four-step Reading Assessment at the heart of *Assess & Progress*, as well as the different photocopiable sheets you can use to record individual, group and class progress.

Photocopiable Reading Assessments for Benchmark Books Stages 3 to 5 – pages 38 to 62

These pages contain one set of photocopiable Reading Assessment record sheets for each Benchmark Book at Oxford Reading Tree Stages 3, 4 and 5 (Book Bands Yellow, Blue and Green).

Find out more – pages 64 – 77

This section presents a range of resources to help you focus on individuals and quickly diagnose any problems, including guidance on how to get the most out of a miscue analysis, and short, specific assessments using Unseen Texts and phonics checklists.

Problems and solutions – pages 78 to 90

Here you can find teaching guidance and activity suggestions to help you repair any problems you've found, and to focus teaching and learning for progress.

If you feel confident about using the Benchmark Book assessments with your class, you can go straight to the Reading Assessments on pages 38–62.

To learn more about carrying out the Benchmark Book Reading Assessments, with real-life examples, turn to page 25.

To find out about more ways to identify the needs of individuals or groups, and next steps learning and teaching guidance, go to page 63.

For practical individual and group progress tracking sheets and reward materials, go to page 92.

Quickstart guide

Assess & Progress follows a simple step-by-step approach, making it easy to integrate into your teaching and learning. It's designed to fit seamlessly into your school's assessment policy, with clear links to National Curriculum levels and Assessing Pupils' Progress.

It will:

- provide evidence of your children's reading achievement
- enable you to make an informed judgement about reading level
- guide you to areas for improvement.

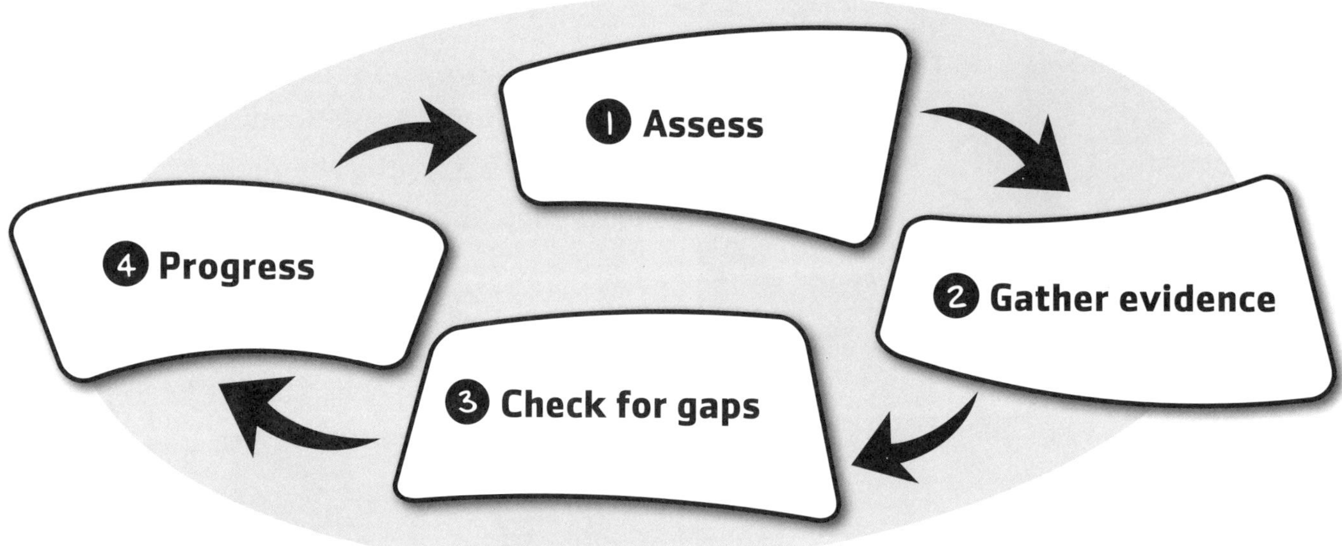

Assess

A one-to-one Reading Assessment using one of the Benchmark Books will give you a clear picture of a child's reading skills and attainment.

Once you have decided to carry out a Reading Assessment with a child, choose a Benchmark Book to read with them. The book should be one step up from their current reading level. For more guidance on when to carry out an assessment and how to choose a book, see page 24.

Use a copy of the book's Reading Assessment (pages 38–62) to carry out the assessment. See page 25 for guidance.

Gather evidence

Alongside the results of a Reading Assessment, you can gather information about children's reading from a variety of activities throughout the school day. This will help you to build up a really three-dimensional picture of their learning. Use *Assess & Progress* to help you collect and reflect on this evidence:

- Record evidence about children during guided or group reading using the Guided Reading Records (pages 92–93).
- Record and track individual progress over time with the Reading Progress Checklists (pages 94–95).
- Build up a detailed picture of your children as readers using short assessments from the **Find out more** section (pages 64–77).
- Collect evidence from a variety of sources and in a variety of forms, using the activity ideas in the **Problems and solutions** section (pages 78–90).

Check for gaps

After reflecting on all the evidence you've gathered, you may want to use the **Find out more** advice and activities (pages 64–77) to confirm what you've found, or to get a close-up view of possible problems.

- Take a closer look at the miscue analysis, to identify the strategies a child is using to read and the kinds of errors they are making.
- Use Unseen Text cards – carefully written, unillustrated texts for Stages 1+ to 11 – to get a close-up view of a child's reading.
- Use the phonics checklists on pages 75–77 to help you pinpoint specific gaps in phonics knowledge and skills.

Progress

Once you've identified where a child is having difficulty, use the **Problems and solutions** guidance on pages 78–90 to help you to fill in the gaps with practical extra support and activity ideas.

The Benchmark Books

Oxford Reading Tree Stages 3–5   Book Bands 3: Yellow–5: Green

Benchmark Book

The Jumble Sale
Story written by Roderick Hunt   Illustrations by Alex Brychta
Mum and Dad have a spring-clean. They take lots of junk, including some of the children's old toys, to a jumble sale. The children are sad. At the jumble sale the children buy back their toys. Mum and Dad are not pleased!
A Biff, Chip and Kipper story.

The Big Match
Story written by Julia Donaldson   Illustrations by Chris Mould
The ducks play the foxes in a football match. Rick Duck and Max Fox both score goals. Max Fox kicks Rick Duck and gets sent off. Rick Duck scores another goal and the ducks win the match!
A Songbirds Phonics story.

The Weather Vane
Story written by Roderick Hunt   Illustrations by Alex Brychta
Wilma and Wilf visit a building site with their Dad. A weather vane arrives at the site and the children jump over it. When the building is finished, the weather vane is fixed to the roof. Biff doesn't believe that Wilf and Wilma have jumped over it … but Wilf has a photograph to prove it!
A Biff, Chip and Kipper story.

Queen Anneena's Feast
Story written by Julia Donaldson   Illustrations by Melanie Williamson
Queen Anneena has invited fifteen queens to her feast. All the queens eat different things, but Queen Teeny Weeny will only eat one green leaf!
A Songbirds Phonics story.

The New Baby
Story written by Roderick Hunt   Illustrations by Alex Brychta
Jo is expecting a baby. Everyone tries to find old baby things for her. At school, the children learn about babies. When Jo's baby is born, Kipper thinks she is great – but doesn't want to help change her nappy!
A Biff, Chip and Kipper story.

Sue Kangaroo
Story written by Julia Donaldson   Illustrations by Daniel Postgate
It's Sue's first day at school. She has fun painting, gluing and playing the spoons. She is upset she can't take the things home with her, but very happy when she learns there's school tomorrow, too!
A Songbirds Phonics story.

Oxford Reading Tree	Book Band*	Reading Recovery Level*	National Curriculum*	Assessing Pupils' Progress*	Scotland	
					Curriculum for Excellence*	5–14*
Stage 3	3: Yellow	6, 7, 8	Level 1C	Low Level 1	First Level	Level A
Stage 3	3: Yellow	6, 7, 8	Level 1C	Low Level 1	First Level	Level A
Stage 4	4: Blue	9, 10, 11	Level 1B	Secure Level 1	First Level	Level A
Stage 4	4: Blue	9, 10, 11	Level 1B	Secure Level 1	First Level	Level A
Stage 5	5: Green	12, 13, 14	Level 1A	High Level 1	First Level	Level A
Stage 5	5: Green	12, 13, 14	Level 1A	High Level 1	First Level	Level A

* Best fit

Assess & Progress and assessing reading

There are two main ways to assess children:

- **Summative assessment** measures what the child already knows. It is a measure of attainment, usually given as a grade or level. This is assessment *of* learning
- **Formative assessment** considers how a child is learning and what they need to learn next. This is assessment *for* learning.

Summative assessment, or assessment *of* learning, allows you to plot the progress children are making from term to term and year to year. It reveals whether children are progressing as you expect them to. It can be used as evidence to support formative assessment, offering a one-off snapshot of a child's (or group's) performance at any given time. *Assess & Progress* enables you to make secure judgements about individual pupil attainment, and to track attainment over time.

Formative assessment, or assessment *for* learning, is at the heart of *Assess & Progress*. It is a way of informing, focusing and enhancing teaching to improve children's progress. The resources in *Assess & Progress* provide a number of different ways to investigate children's individual reading behaviours, and to plan personalized learning paths. These are summarized here.

The Benchmark Books and the four-step Reading Assessment – pages 38 to 62

Every Benchmark Book in *Assess & Progress* has its own four-step Reading Assessment to help you establish the level a child is working at, and to identify their strengths and the areas they need to work on.

Use the Benchmark Book Reading Assessment to work with a child to:

- find out about their attitude to reading
- carry out a miscue analysis to assess reading strategies and behaviours
- investigate their comprehension of what they're reading with questioning linked to assessment focuses
- gather evidence to help you assign their 'best fit' curriculum level
- decide whether they are ready to move on to the next stage of Oxford Reading Tree
- follow up with focused activities to support progress in reading.

Guided Reading Record – pages 92 to 93

This is a practical record sheet that identifies children's achievements
and learning needs in guided and group reading sessions by:

- helping you to focus on specific reading behaviours
- making it easy to record individual attainment.

Reading Progress Checklist – pages 94 to 95

This checklist records individual reading behaviours over time.
It helps you to:

- see the 'stepping-stone' reading behaviours which enable children
  to make progress from one level to the next
- understand strengths and weaknesses
- make an early diagnosis of problems
- set targets for progress.

Find out more – pages 64 to 77

This section provides further short assessments, using simple questions,
miscue analysis, Unseen Text cards or phonics checklists to help you to
get a clearer picture of a child's reading skills. You can use them to:

- confirm strengths and reveal gaps
- pinpoint specific aspects of reading that you think may be
  causing problems
- identify any barriers a child is facing to their reading progress.

Problems and solutions – pages 78 to 90

This section provides practical advice and activities to help you address
problems in reading:

- straightforward suggestions for supporting children's reading progress
- activities to target problems and develop skills
- activities to encourage engagement and motivation.

Finding evidence from continuous assessment

Evidence from continuous assessment helps you to build up a complete picture of where each child is on their personalized reading journey, where they need to go next, and how to get there. You can gather varied evidence about children's reading from across the curriculum throughout the school day.

Here are some suggestions:

- **Children record themselves reading aloud.**
  Take a photo as a child records themselves reading, and use the photo and recording to make a slide presentation. Add a new slide every term to create a multimedia record of their reading.
- **Carry out miscue analyses while children read.**
  Use tracing paper or make a miscue analysis grid. Use the *Assess & Progress* miscue analysis symbols on page 27 to mark strategies and errors on the grid. You can do this with any kind of text.
- **Keep children's written and drawn responses in a reading folder.**
  These might include labels or lists of words; drawings with captions; more extended pieces of writing such as story maps; bookmarks, posters, advertisements or postcards.
- **Take photos or videos of children's responses to a variety of texts and of speaking and listening activities across the curriculum.**
  This might include, for example: children reading their own writing; dance, drama, hot seating or role-play; discussions or debate; model-making or other art work. The photos or videos can be added to slide presentations or saved in pupils' folders on the network.

Assess & Progress and the National Curriculum

***Assess & Progress* is an easy-to-use assessment toolkit for Key Stage 1. It has been developed to support Assessment for Learning (AfL), Assessing Pupils' Progress (APP) and National Curriculum levels.**

Assessment for learning is the process of seeking and interpreting evidence for use by learners and their teachers to decide where the learners are in their learning, where they need to go and how best to get there.

Source: *Assessment for Learning* (Department for Children, Schools and Families)

Assess & Progress enables you to collect and record evidence of children's reading attainment for use as part of assessment for learning. This evidence provides a firm foundation for involving children, other teachers, parents and carers in the assessment for learning process, helping them to understand what it is children need to do to improve, and how they can be supported to become motivated, independent learners. The same evidence helps you to make clear judgements about children's curriculum level, and to plan teaching and learning around their progress.

Assess & Progress and Assessing Pupils' Progress (APP)

Assessing Pupils' Progress (APP) is a structured approach to periodically reviewing children's ongoing work, and matching their attainment to National Curriculum levels. It is based on the Assessment Focuses (AFs) used for National Curriculum assessment.

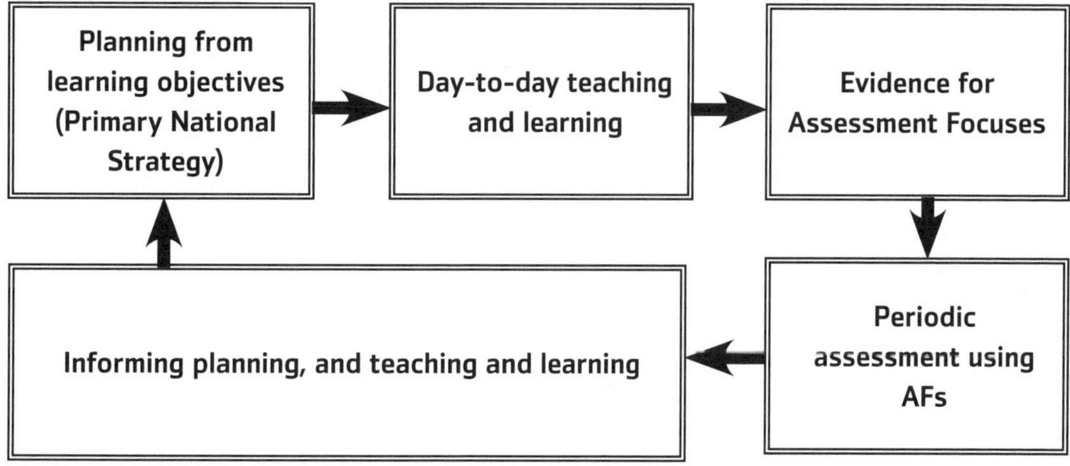

Source: *Assessing Pupils' Progress* (Department for Children, Schools and Families) © Crown copyright 2008

Assess & Progress enables you to check and record children's attainment against the Assessment Focuses, using the *Assess & Progress* Benchmark Book Reading Assessments, the Guided Reading Records and the Reading Progress Checklists. These will help you to reach a fully rounded, evidence-based judgement about a child's National Curriculum level for reading.

The seven Assessment Focuses for reading are:

AF1 use a range of strategies, including accurate decoding of text, to read for meaning

AF2 understand, describe, select or retrieve information, events or ideas from texts and use quotation and reference to text

AF3 deduce, infer or interpret information, events or ideas from texts

AF4 identify and comment on the structure and organisation of texts, including grammatical and presentational features at text level

AF5 explain and comment on writers' uses of language, including grammatical and literary features at word and sentence level

AF6 identify and comment on writers' purposes and viewpoints and the overall effect of the text on the reader

AF7 relate texts to their social, cultural and historical contexts and literary traditions.

Source: *Assessing Pupils' Progress* (2008) Department for Children, Schools and Families
© Crown copyright 2008

The Guided Reading Records and Reading Progress Checklists also show the smaller steps that children take through each National Curriculum level. For example, for AF2, the Level 1 guideline is broken down into three smaller steps:

AF2 Level 1: recalls simple points from familiar texts				
names some characters in a known story, or known characters in a new story	→	recalls some key events in a story	→	retells a story by picking out some significant events

You can use these sheets to record children's attainment in more detail, helping you to see their progression as it happens, to diagnose problems early, and to plan with confidence, making sure that they keep on track.

Assess & Progress **and personalized learning**

Personalized learning is at the heart of Assessment for Learning and Assessing Pupils' Progress. The *Assess & Progress* Benchmark Book Reading Assessment has been carefully designed to support this.
For example, it can be used with a child to:

- check whether they are ready to move on
- investigate any concerns you have about their progress
- find their reading level if they have special needs, speak English as an additional language (EAL) or have just joined your class.

Assess & Progress also helps you work with a child to:

- explore their attitudes to reading and what they know about books
- understand their reading skills and strategies
- find out more about their level of comprehension
- encourage them to self-assess

Assess & Progress and Scotland

***Assess & Progress* is an easy-to-use toolkit for assessing the reading progress of learners as they make the journey through Early and First Level (P1–P3). It supports Assessment is for Learning (AifL) and the principles of Curriculum for Excellence.**

Assess & Progress recognizes that learners use a range of strategies to make meaning from texts. The four-step Reading Assessment enables you to make informed judgements about a child's progress in reading and to ensure that pace and challenge for each learner is appropriate.

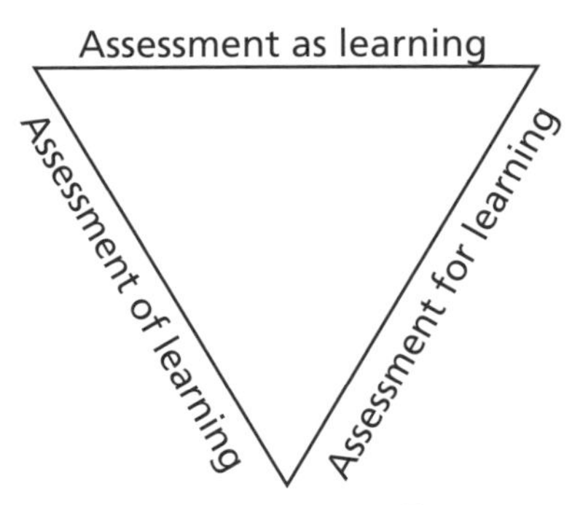

Assessment is for Learning

Assess & Progress allows you to gather evidence on an ongoing basis to get a broad picture of a child's reading progress over time. This creates a firm foundation for the three main concept areas of the Assessment is for Learning triangle.

Assessment as learning

This involves learners reflecting on their own learning through self- and peer assessment and personal learning planning. *Assess & Progress* involves children in taking responsibility for their own learning and identifying areas for improvement. The Reading Assessment gives children the opportunity to discuss their reading strategies and to comment on their performance.

Assessment for learning

This involves considering how a child is learning and what they need to learn next, using formative assessment approaches. Learners are given quality feedback based on clear expectations. *Assess & Progress* helps teachers, parents and carers develop a clear understanding of where children are and how they can improve. The diagnostic tools assist in the setting of success criteria, and on the formulation and sharing of next steps.

Assessment of learning

Here a wide range of evidence is used, including evidence gathered on a day-to-day basis. This information is used to monitor progress and plan for improvement. *Assess & Progress* allows you to make judgements based on sound criteria and reliable assessments. It helps you record evidence over time and ensures consistency throughout your school.

Assess & Progress and Assessment Focuses

Assess & Progress enables you to check and record children's progress against seven Assessment Focuses, using the Benchmark Book Reading Assessments, the Guided Reading Records and the Reading Progress Checklists. The seven Assessment Focuses are closely linked to the evaluative statements made in the Curriculum for Excellence Literacy and English framework.

Assessment Focus	Corresponding Curriculum for Excellence experiences and outcomes (First Level)
AF1	• learning to select and use a range of strategies before, during and after reading to make meaning clear • using knowledge of phonics, context clues, sight vocabulary, punctuation and grammar to read with understanding and expression
AF2	• using knowledge of the features of different types of texts to find, sort and select information for a specific purpose • learning to select and use a range of strategies before, during and after reading to make meaning clear • showing understanding across learning by identifying purpose and main ideas of a text
AF3	• responding to different types of questions and close reading tasks
AF4	• using knowledge of the features of different types of texts to find, sort and select information for a specific purpose • sharing thoughts on structure, characterisation and setting • commenting on effective word choice and other text features
AF5	• commenting on effective word choice and other text features
AF6	• responding to different types of questions and close reading tasks • recognising the author's message and relating it to own experiences
AF7	• appreciating what is special, vibrant and valuable about a variety of languages and cultures • sharing thoughts on structure, characterisation and setting

Assess & Progress and personalized learning

Personalized learning is at the heart of Assessment is for Learning and Assessing Pupils' Progress. The Benchmark Book Reading Assessment can be used with a child to check whether they're ready to move on or any time there is concern about their progress in reading.

Personalization and Choice is a key principle of Scottish curriculum design. *Assess & Progress* will help you respond to individual needs, plan relevant reading programmes and provide appropriate levels of challenge and support through focused diagnostic assessment to help children develop as Successful Learners.

Assess & Progress and Northern Ireland

Assess & Progress is an easy-to-use assessment toolkit for use during the Foundation Stage and Key Stage 1 of the Northern Ireland Curriculum. With Assess & Progress teachers can diagnose reading problems early and plan for improvement with confidence.

"… the central purpose of reading is to gain meaning from print."

Language and Literacy in the Foundation Stage: Reading, Early Years Literacy Interboard Group

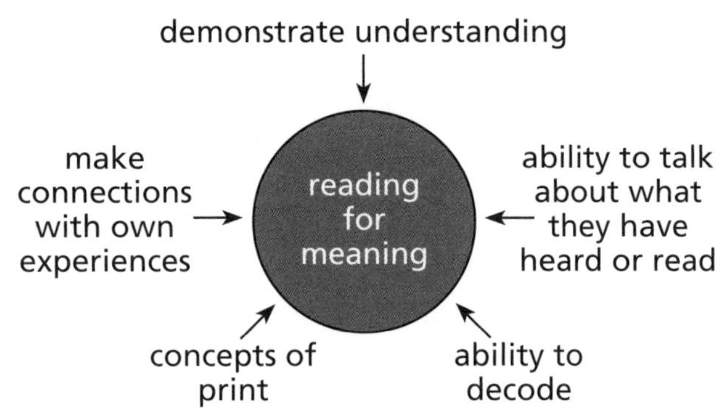

Comprehensive assessment involves collecting information about comprehension as well as ability to decode. *Assess & Progress*'s four-step Reading Assessment enables teachers to assess each of these areas through a reading record and effective questioning, to build up an accurate picture of each child's reading ability.

Assess & Progress and Assessment for Learning

"Through ongoing integrated assessment, teachers build up a comprehensive picture of the progress and learning needs of each child…"

Assessment for Learning, 2007, Northern Ireland Curriculum

Assess & Progress enables you to collect and record evidence of children's reading behaviours for use as part of the continuous learning, teaching, assessment cycle.

Assess & Progress and Assessment of Learning

Assess & Progress helps you gather evidence to track children over time and check that they make the desired progress. In *Better Literacy* (Education and Training Inspectorate (ETI), February 2008), such tracking systems are highlighted as demonstrating "best practice".

Assess & Progress and guided reading

Some children will be ready to work in groups for guided reading
during Year 1 and most children will do so by term 1 of Year 2.
Assess & Progress includes Guided Reading Records for teachers to
record pupils' progress in the skills they need:

- predicting the storyline
- using pictures to tell the story
- using the meaning of text to predict words
- using grammatical knowledge to predict words
- knowing sound/symbol correspondence
- reading some texts independently (with 95% accuracy).

Assess & Progress and setting individual targets

Assess & Progress allows teachers to build up an accurate picture of
the learning needs of each child. It can be used with a child to:

- explore their attitudes to reading and what they know about books
- understand the reading skills and strategies they use
- find out more about their level of comprehension
- encourage them to self-assess
- spot gaps and re-focus their learning.

In this way, teachers can diagnose problems early, and plan for
improvement with confidence.

Assessment Focus	Northern Ireland Curriculum, 2007
AF1	<ul><li>Use a range of reading cues with increasing independence and begin to self correct</li><li>Read on sight some words in a range of meaningful contexts</li><li>Build up a sight vocabulary</li></ul>
AF2	<ul><li>Recognize different types of text and identify specific features of some genres</li><li>Select and use books for specific purposes</li><li>Locate, select and use books for different purposes</li></ul>
AF3	<ul><li>Make and give reasons for predictions</li><li>Use a range of comprehension skills to interpret and discuss texts</li><li>Begin to use evidence from texts, e.g. predicting, inferring and deducing</li></ul>
AF4	<ul><li>Recognize different types of text and identify specific features of some genres</li><li>Use extended vocabulary when discussing texts</li><li>Explore and begin to understand how texts are structured in a range of genres</li></ul>
AF5	<ul><li>Recognize different types of text and identify specific features of some genres</li><li>Talk about ways in which the language is written down … identifying the features of written language</li></ul>
AF6	<ul><li>Express opinions and give reasons based on what they have read</li></ul>
AF7	<ul><li>Be aware of own cultural heritage, its traditions and celebrations (Personal Development and Mutual Understanding, KS1)</li></ul>

Source: *Northern Ireland Curriculum,* Foundation and KS1

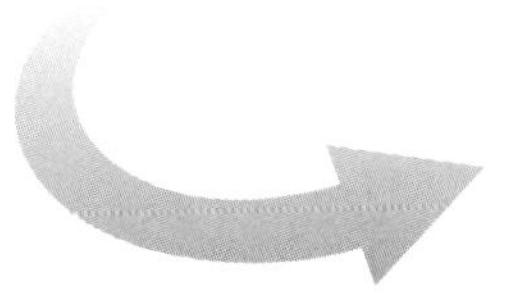

Assess & Progress and Wales

Assess & Progress helps teachers gather evidence for assessment of children's reading attainment to support planning for progression. It enables teachers to make informed judgments about expected learning outcomes and plan learning opportunities based on individual progress.

With the implementation of the Foundation Phase in Wales the need for children to be supported in their reading is as great as ever. The Welsh Assembly Government guidance states that "Opportunities throughout the Foundation Phase should enable children to enjoy reading and to make progress in their ability…" (*Framework for Children's Learning for 3 to 7-year-olds in Wales* (2008) Welsh Assembly Government).

A key principle of the Foundation Phase is that children progress at different rates and move on when they are developmentally ready. To achieve this aim, teachers assess individual pupil progress to ensure that learning opportunities are tailored to suit the learner's needs. *Assess & Progress* is an easy-to-use assessment toolkit for children in the Foundation Phase who are ready to learn how to read, and who have already made some steps towards reading independently.

At Oxford Reading Tree Stages 3 – 5, children in the Foundation Phase should be achieving the Foundation Phase Outcome 4 where children "recognize familiar words in simple texts and when reading aloud, use their knowledge of letters and sound-symbol relationships to read words and establish meaning" (*Framework for Children's Learning for 3 to 7-year-olds in Wales*).

In the Foundation Phase children are expected to:

- read with enjoyment and increasing fluency, accuracy, understanding and independence, building on what they already know, including:
  - the sounds and names of the alphabet
  - an awareness of the sounds of spoken language
  - the use of various approaches to word identification and recognition
  - the use of their understanding of grammatical structure and the meaning of the text as a whole to make sense of print
- understand and respond to stories and poems, and in particular to:
  - talk about characters, events and language and use appropriate terminology
  - explain the content of a passage or whole text
  - review their reading with a practitioner
- explore meaning within a book as a whole:
  - using their knowledge of book conventions, story structure, patterns of language and presentational devices, and their background knowledge and understanding of the content of a book
  - keeping the overall sense of a passage in mind as a checking device
  - recognizing the structural devices for organizing information, for example contents, headings, captions.

Source: *Language, Literacy and Communication Skills* (2008) Welsh Assembly Government

In addition the Oxford Reading Tree *Assess & Progress* toolkit enables teachers to assess criteria in the Skills Framework, particularly in Reading.

Locating, selecting and using information using reading strategies
- Decode text and begin to find information using organizational devices and available clues to deduce meaning.
- Use a range of word identification skills and different strategies to locate and reorganize ideas and information from different sources.
- Use different reading strategies to locate, select and summarize information, identifying accurately the key points.

Responding to what has been read
- Respond to what is read, expressing opinions about major events or ideas and making connections between reading and own experiences.
- Confirm their understanding by responding to texts orally and/or in writing, and taking into account the opinions of others.
- Discuss and evaluate texts, using inference and deduction where necessary and considering carefully the interpretations of others.

Source: *Skills Framework for 3 to 19-year-olds in Wales* (2008) Welsh Assembly Government

How to use *Assess & Progress* in the classroom

You can use the different assessment resources in *Assess & Progress* flexibly according to your needs, the needs of your children and your school's assessment policy. All assessment takes a little time and involves observing your children closely.

Decide when to do a Benchmark Book Reading Assessment

You can use the Reading Assessment when:

- you think a child may be ready to move up to the next Oxford Reading Tree stage or the next Book Band
- you have concerns about a child's progress and want to identify any problem areas
- you want to check children's reading attainment and progress.

If you are using the Reading Assessment to check and record progress, you might choose to carry it out:

- with all children once a term
- with a representative child from each reading group every half-term, choosing a different child each time (this means that every child will have at least one *Assess & Progress* Reading Assessment during the year).

Whichever route you choose, the four-step Reading Assessment is a substantial piece of evidence to help form and support your professional judgement about a child's attainment and progress in reading.

Find the right Benchmark Book

Each Benchmark Book represents the *starting point* in an Oxford Reading Tree stage.

For children using Oxford Reading Tree as a core reading resource
To test readiness to move on, choose a Benchmark Book from the stage above the one the child is currently reading. For example, if you think a child is reading confidently at Stage 4, check their readiness to move on using a Stage 5 Benchmark Book.

For children not using Oxford Reading Tree as a core reading resource
Identify the Book Band, Reading Recovery level or curriculum level that best fits their current reading. Use the chart on pages 10–11 to choose a Benchmark Book at the next step up. For example, if a child is reading at Blue Book Band, check their readiness to move on by using a Benchmark Book at Green Book Band.

Carry out the Reading Assessment

The four-step Reading Assessment involves working one-to-one with the child, and will take around 20 minutes to complete. Make sure you carry out the assessment in a quiet place where the child will feel comfortable reading.

The four steps of the Reading Assessment are:

- **Step 1 Prior knowledge**   finding out what the child knows before they begin reading
- **Step 2 Oral reading**   using a miscue analysis to gather detailed information on reading
- **Step 3 Comprehension**   having a conversation to find out what the child understands
- **Step 4 Summary**   creating a quick-reference record of skills, attainment and targets.

These four steps are described here, alongside a real-life example of a Reading Assessment carried out by NFER. In the example, Laura has been reading *Biff, Chip and Kipper* books at Stage 2. Her teacher wants to know if Laura is ready to read at Stage 3, and carries out a Reading Assessment with Stage 3 Benchmark Book *The Jumble Sale*.

> There are more real-life examples of Reading Assessments in the Examples area of the *Assess & Progress* software. These Examples show how you can draw out and recognize valuable information about reading behaviours during each step of the Reading Assessment, and how to get the best from this powerful assessment.

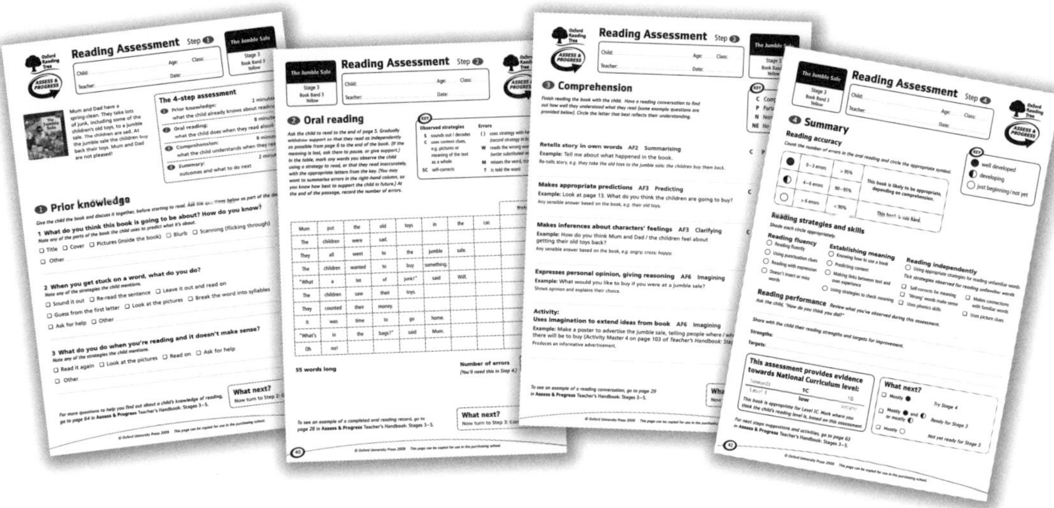

① Prior knowledge

Before you start to read, discuss the Benchmark Book with the child. Use this as an opportunity to find out what the child knows about their own reading skills, and to activate their prior knowledge using the clues that the title and cover give to the book's content. Prompt questions are provided in Step 1 of the Reading Assessment. As the child talks, tick off the skills and strategies they mention.

I hope you are going to enjoy this book we are going to read.

Have a look. What can you see in the picture?

What do you think the story is going to be about?

Kipper.

Where is Kipper?

At a shop.

Try and look at this title.

Jumble... Sale.

Do you know what a jumble sale is?

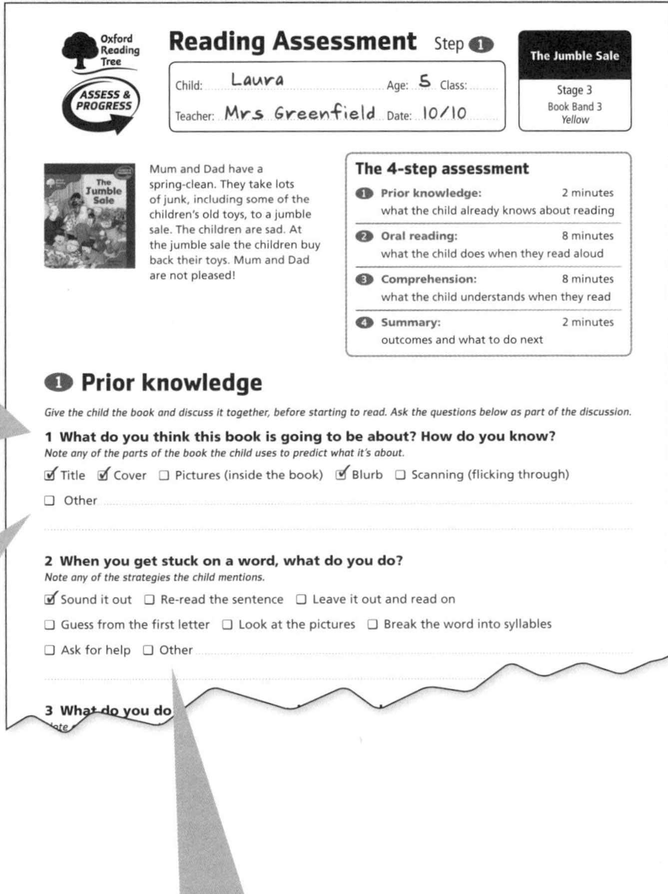

What could we read before we open the book?

The back of the book.

The back of the book – yes and what's that called? Do you remember?

[Shakes head]

It's called the blurb.

What about when you're reading, what do you do if you don't know a word?

Sound it out.

Is there anything that worries you when you're reading?

No.

② **Oral reading**

Step 2 involves listening closely to the child as they read aloud a section of text from the Benchmark Book, and completing a miscue analysis to identify key strategies and common errors the child makes while they read. Points (a)–(c) below explain how to do this.

(a) Read up to the beginning of the miscue analysis section
Start reading the Benchmark Book together. Gradually withdraw your support as far as possible, to allow the child to read as independently as they can from the beginning of the miscue analysis text.

(b) The child reads the text, you record strategies and errors
As the child reads the section, carefully follow what they read using the miscue analysis chart. The words they read correctly (and without using any obvious strategy) you can tick or leave blank.

Words you observe the child using a strategy to read successfully, or words they make an error in reading, should be marked using the symbols in the key.

> The symbols for observed strategies are:
> **S**   for sounding out or decoding out loud
> **C**   for using context clues such as the meaning of the sentence or the pictures
> **SC**   for self-correcting

These symbols will create a record of the strategies the child is using to read the unfamiliar words in the text. They do not count as errors, unless you help the child to use them. If you do give support, record the strategy symbol inside brackets to show it counts as an error.

> The symbols for observed errors are:
> **(S)**   for sounding out with support
> **(C)**   for using context clues with support
> **(SC)**   for self-correcting with support
> **W**   for reading the wrong word (also write in the word they substituted)
> **M**   for missing out a word (or saying it so it can't be heard), and moving on
> **T**   for when you tell the child what the word is

If in doubt, record what the child actually says while you are completing the miscue analysis, then return afterwards to analyse precisely what the child's strategies and mistakes were.

Allow the child time to try and work out a word or to self-correct, but step in before they get upset or frustrated. The aim is to gather information about their reading, so they shouldn't feel any pressure. Also be sure to give support if the child has lost the sense of the text, even if they continue to read.

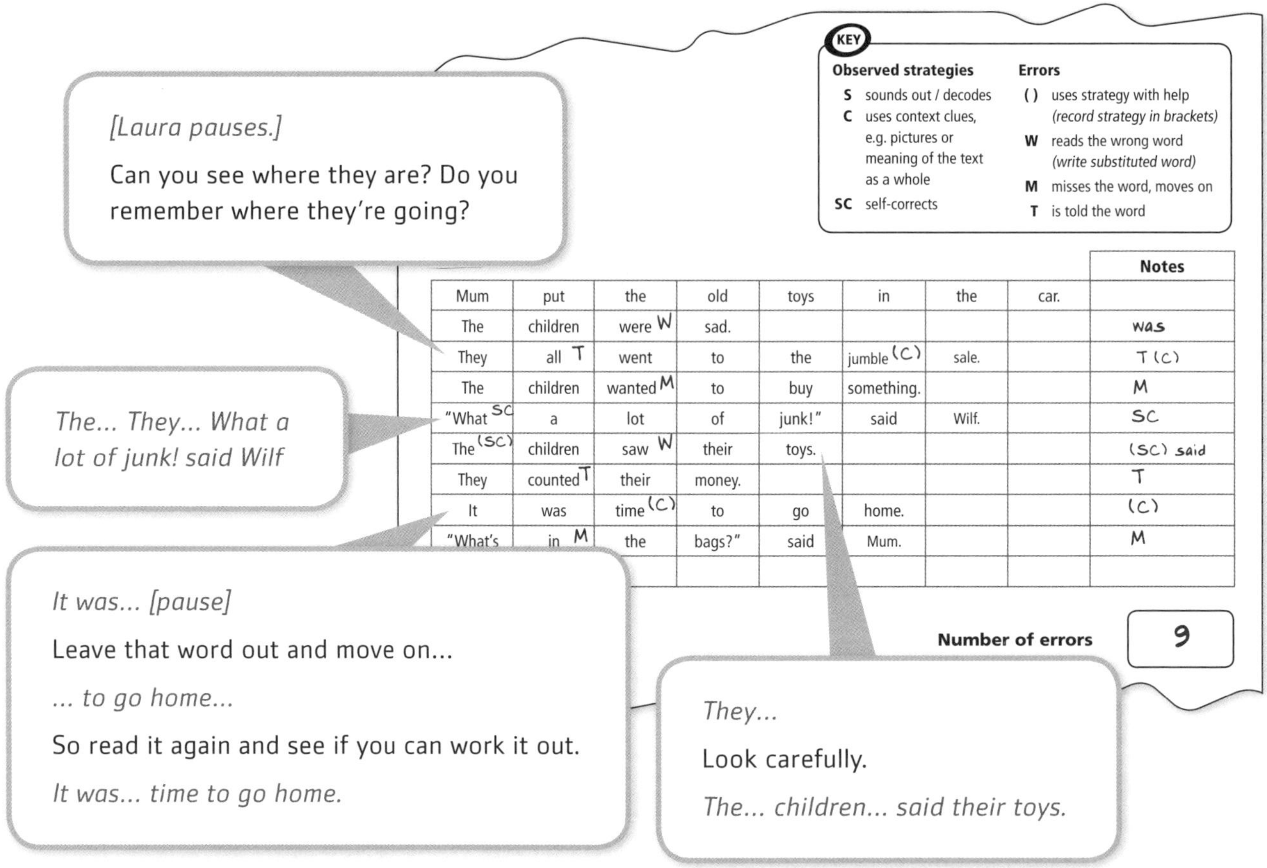

KEY

Observed strategies		Errors	
S	sounds out / decodes	( )	uses strategy with help (record strategy in brackets)
C	uses context clues, e.g. pictures or meaning of the text as a whole	W	reads the wrong word (write substituted word)
SC	self-corrects	M	misses the word, moves on
		T	is told the word

								Notes
Mum	put	the	old	toys	in	the	car.	
The	children	were W	sad.					was
They	all T	went	to	the	jumble (C)	sale.		T (C)
The	children	wanted M	to	buy	something.			M
"What SC	a	lot	of	junk!"	said	Wilf.		SC
The (SC)	children	saw W	their	toys.				(SC) said
They	counted T	their	money.					T
It	was	time (C)	to	go	home.			(C)
"What's	in M	the	bags?"	said	Mum.			M

Number of errors   9

(c) Record the number of errors

After you have finished reading (the instructions for Step 3 tell you how far through the book you need to read), return to the miscue analysis to count up the number of errors and record it in the box at the foot of the page.

You'll need this information to complete the reading accuracy table in Step 4, which shows the percentage accuracy of the child's reading. Generally, to be ready to read at the level of the Benchmark Book, the child should be able to read it with over 90% accuracy and with good comprehension. They will feel more comfortable still if they are able to read it with about 95% accuracy – this is widely believed to be the most effective instructional level for teaching reading.

3 Comprehension

Comprehension of the book should emerge as naturally as possible. Have a conversation to share views and opinions about it, either while the child is reading, or when they have finished. Follow up any comments the child makes, and ask them to explain, give an opinion or predict what might happen.

Prompt questions matched to Assessment Focuses and key comprehension skills are provided in Step 3, along with points to look for in the child's answers. These should help you to guide the conversation, and judge the level of understanding shown by the child. Ask alternative or additional questions where appropriate in order to gather all the information you need to make a good judgement about the child's level of comprehension.

The last question in Step 3 takes the form of a follow-up activity based on the book. This offers another way to explore a child's comprehension, and helps you to build up evidence of different types.

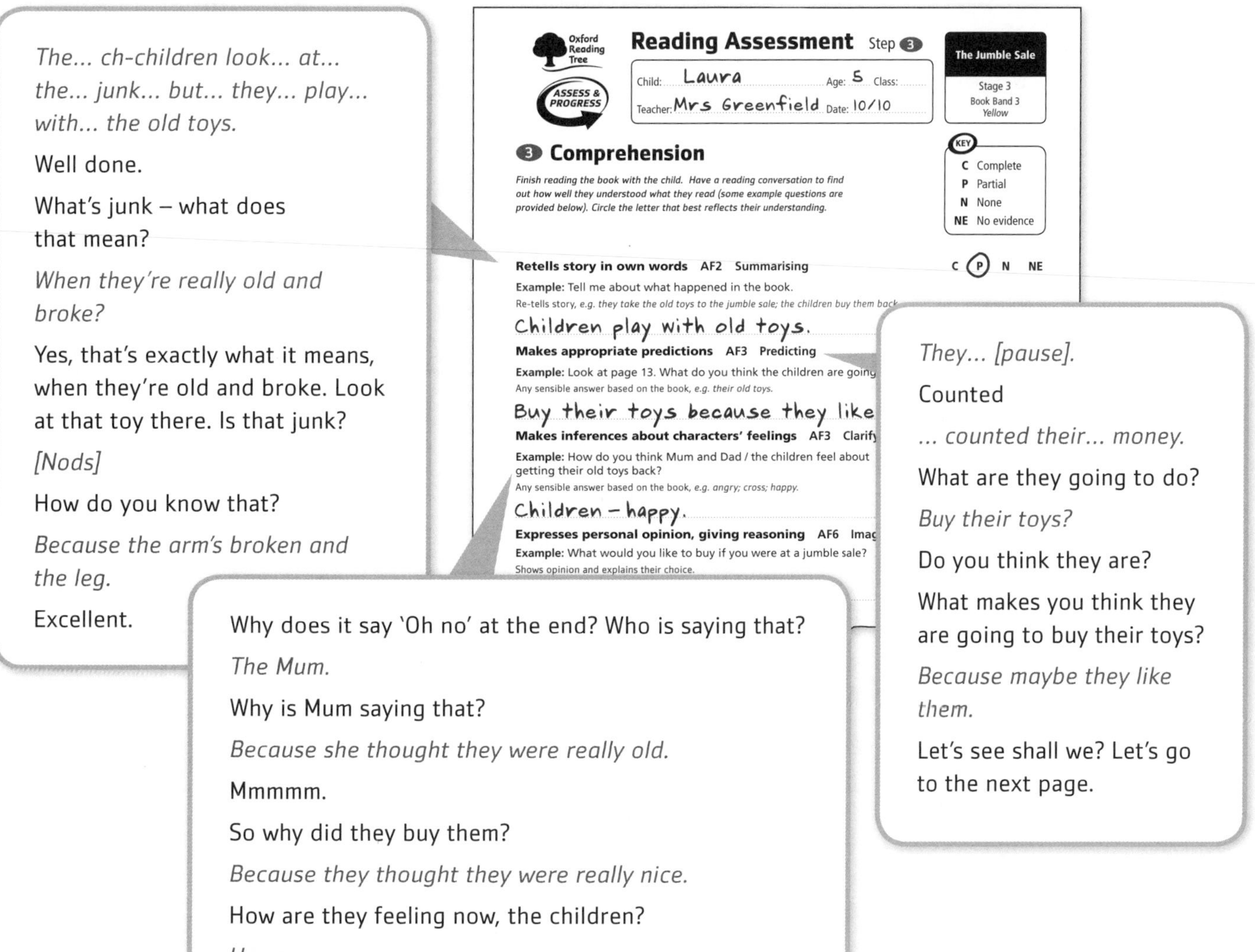

4 Summary

The summary page draws together all the information you have gained from the Reading Assessment. Use it to:

- record how accurate the the child's reading was
- summarize their strategies and skills
- make an overall judgement of their reading level
- decide whether they are ready to move on.

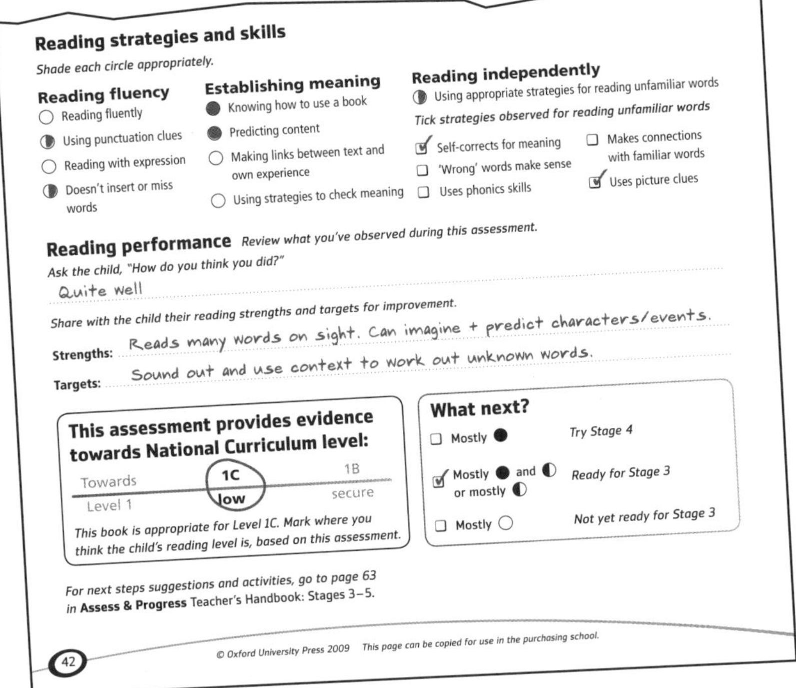

You can also use this as an opportunity to discuss their own reading performance with the child. There is space to record their self-assessment, and the strengths and future targets you agree together.

When filling in the circles in the reading strategies and skills section, shade as much as you think is appropriate (that is, you don't need to follow the key exactly).

When you decide on the child's overall reading level, remember to take into account all aspects of the child's assessment:

- how familiar they are with the different features of a book
- their reading accuracy
- their reading comprehension.

If a child does extremely well in all areas of the Reading Assessment, you may want to try assessing their readiness to read at the *next* level up. For example, if a child performs exceptionally in the Reading Assessment for Stage 5, try assessing them again using the Benchmark Book for Stage 6. The Reading Assessment helps you judge if moving up two levels gives the child the appropriate degree of support and challenge.

Look at all the steps in the Reading Assessment to identify specific areas for improvement and future reading targets. Use this as the basis for your professional judgement on whether the child is ready to read at the level of the Benchmark Book.

Guided Reading Record – pages 92 to 93

A Guided Reading Record enables you to record evidence about children in a reading group quickly and clearly.

Each Guided Reading Record covers all the assessment focuses (AF1–7) for one curriculum level, broken down into smaller steps to show progress.

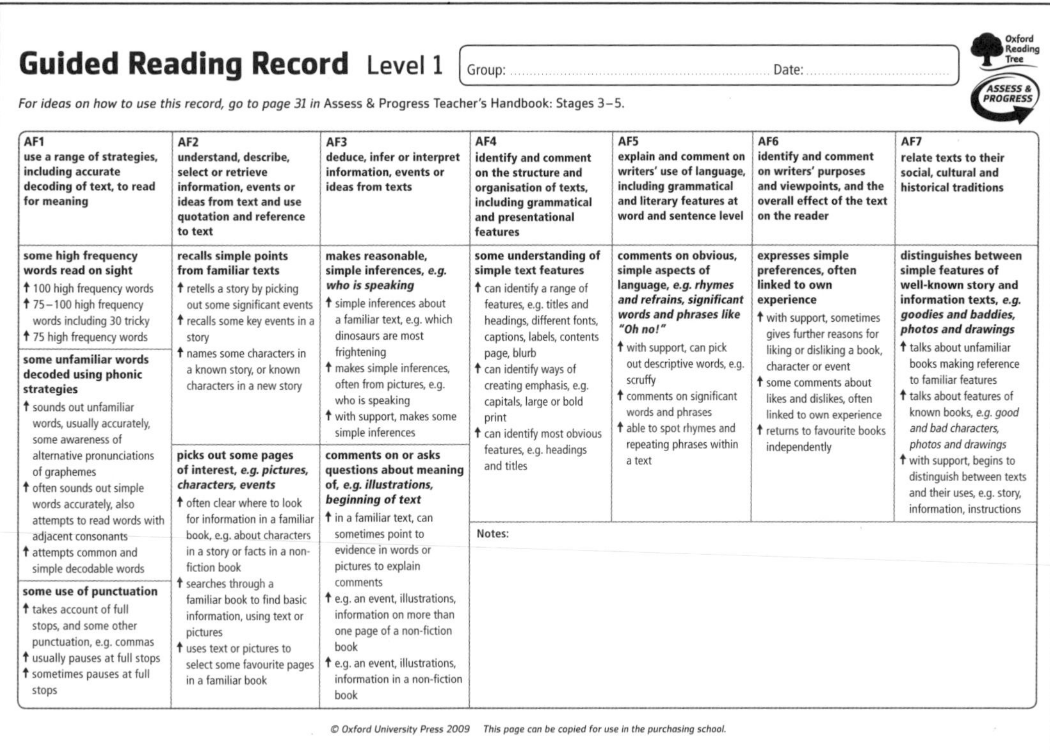

The form reproduced is a table:

AF1 use a range of strategies, including accurate decoding of text, to read for meaning	AF2 understand, describe, select or retrieve information, events or ideas from text and use quotation and reference to text	AF3 deduce, infer or interpret information, events or ideas from texts	AF4 identify and comment on the structure and organisation of texts, including grammatical and presentational features	AF5 explain and comment on writers' use of language, including grammatical and literary features at word and sentence level	AF6 identify and comment on writers' purposes and viewpoints, and the overall effect of the text on the reader	AF7 relate texts to their social, cultural and historical traditions
some high frequency words read on sight ↑ 100 high frequency words ↑ 75–100 high frequency words including 30 tricky ↑ 75 high frequency words **some unfamiliar words decoded using phonic strategies** ↑ sounds out unfamiliar words, usually accurately, some awareness of alternative pronunciations of graphemes ↑ often sounds out simple words accurately, also attempts to read words with adjacent consonants ↑ attempts common and simple decodable words	**recalls simple points from familiar texts** ↑ retells a story by picking out some significant events ↑ recalls some key events in a story ↑ names some characters in a known story, or known characters in a new story	**makes reasonable, simple inferences, e.g. who is speaking** ↑ simple inferences about a familiar text, e.g. which dinosaurs are most frightening ↑ makes simple inferences, often from pictures, e.g. who is speaking ↑ with support, makes some simple inferences	**some understanding of simple text features** ↑ can identify a range of features, e.g. titles and headings, different fonts, captions, labels, contents page, blurb ↑ can identify ways of creating emphasis, e.g. capitals, large or bold print ↑ can identify most obvious features, e.g. headings and titles	**comments on obvious, simple aspects of language, e.g. rhymes and refrains, significant words and phrases like "Oh no!"** ↑ with support, can pick out descriptive words, e.g. scruffy ↑ comments on significant words and phrases ↑ able to spot rhymes and repeating phrases within a text	**expresses simple preferences, often linked to own experience** ↑ with support, sometimes gives further reasons for liking or disliking a book, character or event ↑ some comments about likes and dislikes, often linked to own experience ↑ returns to favourite books independently	**distinguishes between simple features of well-known story and information texts, e.g. goodies and baddies, photos and drawings** ↑ talks about unfamiliar books making reference to familiar features ↑ talks about features of known books, e.g. good and bad characters, photos and drawings ↑ with support, begins to distinguish between texts and their uses, e.g. story, information, instructions
some use of punctuation ↑ takes account of full stops, and some other punctuation, e.g. commas ↑ usually pauses at full stops ↑ sometimes pauses at full stops	**picks out some pages of interest, e.g. pictures, characters, events** ↑ often clear where to look for information in a familiar book, e.g. about characters in a story or facts in a non-fiction book ↑ searches through a familiar book to find basic information, using text or pictures ↑ uses text or pictures to select some favourite pages in a familiar book	**comments on or asks questions about meaning of, e.g. illustrations, beginning of text** ↑ in a familiar text, can sometimes point to evidence in words or pictures to explain comments ↑ e.g. an event, illustrations, information on more than one page of a non-fiction book ↑ e.g. an event, illustrations, information in a non-fiction book	Notes:			

© Oxford University Press 2009   This page can be copied for use in the purchasing school.

When you plan your guided reading session, choose one Assessment Focus as a target for the session. It may reflect skills you're focusing on in shared reading or the particular needs of the group.

- Highlight or circle the target guideline on the sheet, to refer to during the reading session.
- As you guide the group in reading and discussing the text, keep the target skills in mind.
- During or immediately after the session, make brief notes about your observations.

The completed Guided Reading Record helps you compare progress across the group for the target behaviour. By targeting the same Assessment Focus over several sessions, you'll be able to see which children are making progress and which need more support.

Reading Progress Checklist – pages 94 to 95

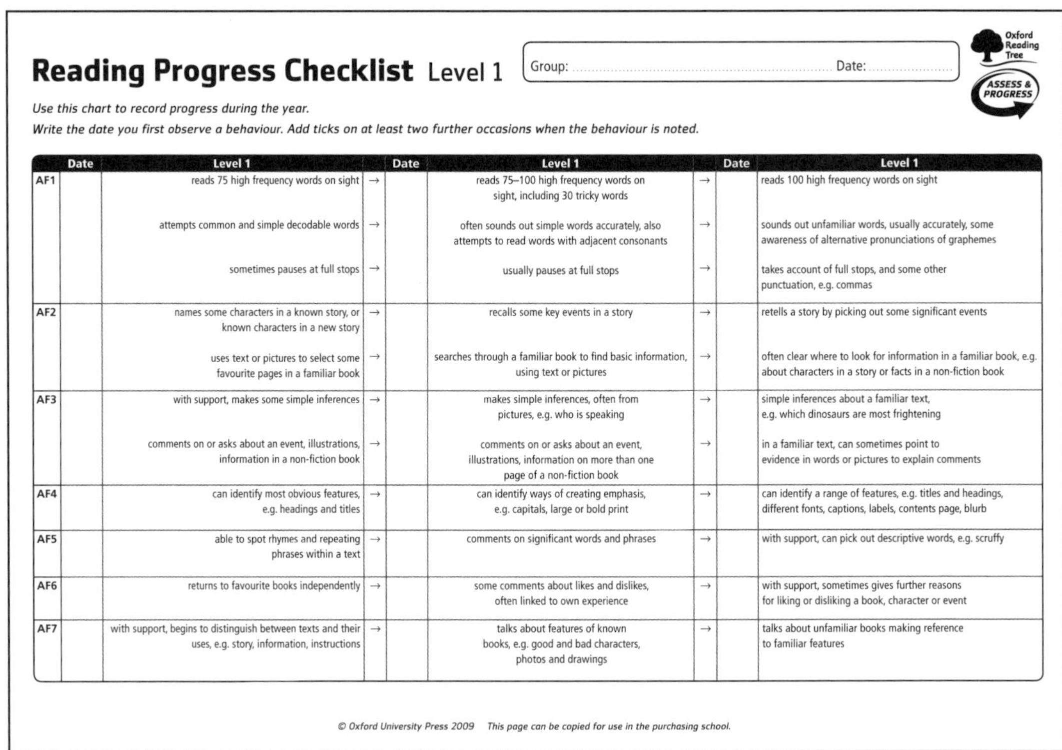

Reading Progress Checklist Level 1 — Group: .... Date: ....

Oxford Reading Tree — ASSESS & PROGRESS

Use this chart to record progress during the year.

Write the date you first observe a behaviour. Add ticks on at least two further occasions when the behaviour is noted.

	Date	Level 1		Date	Level 1		Date	Level 1
AF1		reads 75 high frequency words on sight	→		reads 75–100 high frequency words on sight, including 30 tricky words	→		reads 100 high frequency words on sight
		attempts common and simple decodable words	→		often sounds out simple words accurately, also attempts to read words with adjacent consonants	→		sounds out unfamiliar words, usually accurately, some awareness of alternative pronunciations of graphemes
		sometimes pauses at full stops	→		usually pauses at full stops	→		takes account of full stops, and some other punctuation, e.g. commas
AF2		names some characters in a known story, or known characters in a new story	→		recalls some key events in a story	→		retells a story by picking out some significant events
		uses text or pictures to select some favourite pages in a familiar book	→		searches through a familiar book to find basic information, using text or pictures	→		often clear where to look for information in a familiar book, e.g. about characters in a story or facts in a non-fiction book
AF3		with support, makes some simple inferences	→		makes simple inferences, often from pictures, e.g. who is speaking	→		simple inferences about a familiar text, e.g. which dinosaurs are most frightening
		comments on or asks about an event, illustrations, information in a non-fiction book	→		comments on or asks about an event, illustrations, information on more than one page of a non-fiction book	→		in a familiar text, can sometimes point to evidence in words or pictures to explain comments
AF4		can identify most obvious features, e.g. headings and titles	→		can identify ways of creating emphasis, e.g. capitals, large or bold print	→		can identify a range of features, e.g. titles and headings, different fonts, captions, labels, contents page, blurb
AF5		able to spot rhymes and repeating phrases within a text	→		comments on significant words and phrases	→		with support, can pick out descriptive words, e.g. scruffy
AF6		returns to favourite books independently	→		some comments about likes and dislikes, often linked to own experience	→		with support, sometimes gives further reasons for liking or disliking a book, character or event
AF7		with support, begins to distinguish between texts and their uses, e.g. story, information, instructions	→		talks about features of known books, e.g. good and bad characters, photos and drawings	→		talks about unfamiliar books making reference to familiar features

© Oxford University Press 2009   This page can be copied for use in the purchasing school.

You can track individual children's progress across levels using a Reading Progress Checklist. It lists the same steps in progression as the Guided Reading Record, but allows you to record across all Assessment Focuses and over time.

Use this checklist for recording progress:
- routinely for individual children
- routinely for a representative child from each reading group
- as needed, for children you may have concerns about.

Class tracking charts – pages 96 to 97

The class tracking charts help you to record progress for your whole class over the year.

- The **Reading Assessment Class Tracking Chart** helps you summarize the results of all the *Assess & Progress* Benchmark Book Reading Assessments you have carried out.

Reading Assessment Class Tracking Chart   Group: .... Date: ....

Use this chart to summarize the results of your class's Benchmark Book Reading Assessments.

Name	Date	Curriculum level	Oxford Reading Tree Stage / Book Band	Notes

- The **Class Reading Progress Chart** allows you to record progress through curriculum levels for all the children in your class over the year.

Each term you can fill in the relevant row, writing names or initials in the box under the appropriate level. You can then repeat the process the following term. Most children should move forwards two or three boxes during each school year.

Class Reading Progress Chart   Group: .... Date: ....

Use this chart to record your class's progress during the year.
When you assess children, write their names or initials in the appropriate space.
The shaded areas show you average attainment for reading in Year 1.

	Early Learning Goals			National Curriculum Level					
	working towards / within	working securely within	working beyond	1C	1B	1A	2C	2B	2A
Year 1 Autumn term									
Year 1 Spring term									
Year 1 Summer term									

Training and resources software

The training and resources software provides:

- a click-through **Training presentation,** including video clips
- an **Examples** area showing how real-life Reading Assessments have been carried out
- **Feedback and reward resources,** including template certificates and a bank of *Assess & Progress* clip-art
- editable versions of all the **Reading Assessments and record sheets** so you can adapt resources to suit your needs.

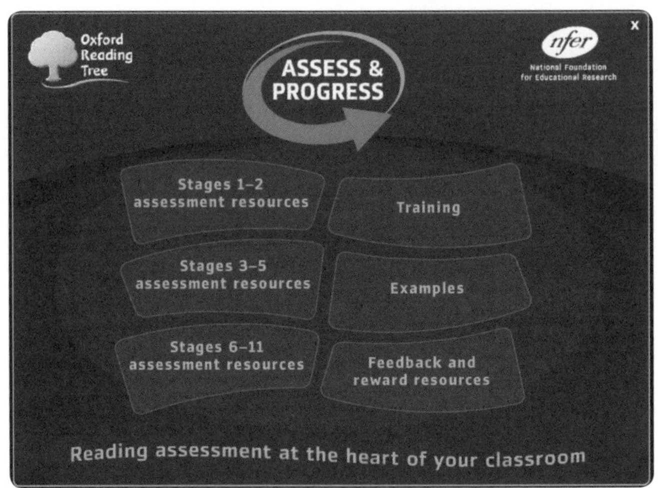

Also included are:

- text-only versions of the Benchmark Books and Phonics Benchmark Card – in case you want to check a child's ability to read without support from pictures
- all the Reading Assessments for the Benchmark Books, including separate versions for use with other curricula, including Scotland's Curriculum for Excellence
- a blank Reading Assessment, to adapt and use with texts of your choice
- all the Unseen Text cards and the record sheets to go with them
- the phonics checklists
- the Guided Reading Records
- the Reading Progress Checklists
- the Reading Assessment Class Tracking Chart
- the Class Reading Progress Chart.

Interpreting the evidence

The more evidence you have about a child's reading, the more accurate your assessment of their progress will be. *Assess & Progress* provides two main types of evidence – from the Benchmark Book Reading Assessment and from continuous assessment.

Evidence from the Benchmark Book Reading Assessment

Step 4 of the Reading Assessment summarizes what you have found out from reading the Benchmark Book with the child. It provides a snapshot of strategies used by the child, their strengths and weaknesses, their understanding of the text, their readiness to read at the level of the Benchmark Book, and the approximate curriculum level they are working at.

Evidence from continuous assessment

Evidence from continuous assessment may include lots of different types of information (see page 14 for some ideas). You can use the Reading Progress Checklist (pages 94–95) to summarize what you've learnt about a child's reading.

Combining the evidence

You can use Step 4 of the Benchmark Book Reading Assessment (the Summary) and the Reading Progress Checklist to combine and compare all the evidence. This evidence can be shared with the child's next teacher, and will be helpful in discussions with parents or senior teachers.

If the evidence is consistent and the child is making good progress
They are ready to work at the level of the Benchmark Book.

If the evidence is consistent but the child is not making good progress
Look at the patterns of errors. For example, does the child:
- Use phonics confidently?
- Stumble on high frequency words?
- Miss out, mumble over or hurry past words?
- Have strategies they use to attempt to read a word they're unsure of? (Do they wait for help?)
- Guess at answers to comprehension questions?
- Understand the story, beyond the information given in the text? (Can they make simple inferences?)

- Understand language patterns and how stories work?
- Recognize words or language patterns they have met before?
- Make reasonable predictions about the text, and use their prior knowledge to support their reading?

If you want to confirm what the problem is or narrow it down further, the **Find out more** section (pages 64–77) contains advice and resources to help you.

The **Problems and solutions** section (pages 78–90) provides advice and activities to help you repair problems and overcome barriers to reading. A list of common problems covered is on page 78.

If the evidence is not consistent
Continuous assessment will usually give the most accurate overall picture, as it's made up of different types of evidence gathered over time. For a variety of reasons, the Reading Assessment may not reflect the child's normal reading performance. For example:

- they may have been affected by external factors such as health, emotional or social difficulties, and home circumstances
- they weren't comfortable reading one-to-one
- the Benchmark Book didn't hold their interest
- they've already heard or read the Benchmark Book, so 'out-performed'
- they've suddenly experienced success with reading, and their motivation has increased.

If the evidence is confused, you may want to do another Reading Assessment using a different Benchmark Book or one of the Unseen Text cards at a similar level (see **Reassessing children** on page 91. If you can't identify a specific problem, you can use the short **Find out more** assessments (pages 64–77) to investigate.

Finding a level

With evidence from both the Reading Assessment and continuous assessment, you'll be in a good position to make a judgement about a child's level of attainment. Since most children show a range of attainment across different reading behaviours, use the Assessment Focus guidelines in the Guided Reading Records on pages 92–93 to identify the behaviours that best describe the child's reading, and help you reach an overall level judgement.

There are various ways of recording your children's attainment over time to track their progress. You can use the Class Reading Progress Chart on page 97, for example, or resources for Assessing Pupils' Progress, or your school's own system. By tracking over time, you'll see whether children are progressing at an appropriate rate according to your school's assessment policy.

If any of your children are making slower progress than you'd expect, think about:

- investigating further (see the **Find out more** section on pages 64–77)
- providing teaching support and activities that help to develop target skills and knowledge (see the **Problems and solutions** section on pages 78–90)
- consulting with your special needs teacher to decide whether specialist intervention is needed.

Reading Assessments for the Benchmark Books

This section contains a photocopiable four-step Reading Assessment for each of the Benchmark Books at Oxford Reading Tree Stages 3–5 (Book Bands Yellow, Blue and Green). There are also editable and printable versions of these on the *Assess & Progress* software. Go to the **Assessment resources** area for Stages 3–5, then to the relevant stage number.

The table below shows levels for each of the Benchmark Books for Oxford Reading Tree Stages 3–5, and the page numbers in this handbook for their Reading Assessments.

Benchmark Book	Oxford Reading Tree	Book Band*	Reading Recovery Level*	Reading Assessment on pages
The Jumble Sale	Stage 3	3: Yellow	6, 7, 8	39–42
The Big Match	Stage 3	3: Yellow	6, 7, 8	43–46
The Weather Vane	Stage 4	4: Blue	9, 10, 11	47–50
Queen Anneena's Feast	Stage 4	4: Blue	9, 10, 11	51–54
The New Baby	Stage 5	5: Green	12, 13, 14	55–58
Sue Kangaroo	Stage 5	5: Green	12, 13, 14	59–62

*** Best fit**

Reading Assessment Step ❶

Child: .... Age: .... Class: ....

Teacher: .... Date: ....

Mum and Dad have a spring-clean. They take lots of junk, including some of the children's old toys, to a jumble sale. The children are sad. At the jumble sale the children buy back their toys. Mum and Dad are not pleased!

The 4-step assessment

❶ **Prior knowledge:**   2 minutes
what the child already knows about reading

❷ **Oral reading:**   8 minutes
what the child does when they read aloud

❸ **Comprehension:**   8 minutes
what the child understands when they read

❹ **Summary:**   2 minutes
outcomes and what to do next

❶ Prior knowledge

Give the child the book and discuss it together, before starting to read. Ask the questions below as part of the discussion.

1 What do you think this book is going to be about? How do you know?
Note any of the parts of the book the child uses to predict what it's about.

☐ Title   ☐ Cover   ☐ Pictures (inside the book)   ☐ Blurb   ☐ Scanning (flicking through)

☐ Other ....

....

2 When you get stuck on a word, what do you do?
Note any of the strategies the child mentions.

☐ Sound it out   ☐ Re-read the sentence   ☐ Leave it out and read on

☐ Guess from the first letter   ☐ Look at the pictures   ☐ Break the word into syllables

☐ Ask for help   ☐ Other ....

....

3 What do you do when you're reading and it doesn't make sense?
Note any of the strategies the child mentions.

☐ Read it again   ☐ Look at the pictures   ☐ Read on   ☐ Ask for help

☐ Other ....

....

For more questions to help you find out about a child's knowledge of reading, go to page 64 in **Assess & Progress** *Teacher's Handbook: Stages 3–5.*

What next?

Now turn to Step 2: **Oral reading**

Reading Assessment Step ❷

Oxford Reading Tree

ASSESS & PROGRESS

Child: .... Age: .... Class: ....

Teacher: .... Date: ....

❷ Oral reading

Ask the child to read to the end of page 5. Gradually withdraw support so that they read as independently as possible from page 6 to the end of the book. (If the meaning is lost, ask them to pause, or give support.) In the table, mark any words you observe the child using a strategy to read, or that they read inaccurately, with the appropriate letters from the key. (You may want to summarise errors in the right-hand column, so you know how best to support the child in future.) At the end of the passage, record the number of errors.

KEY

Observed strategies	**Errors**
S sounds out / decodes	**( )** uses strategy with help *(record strategy in brackets)*
C uses context clues, e.g. pictures or meaning of the text as a whole	**W** reads the wrong word *(write substituted word)*
SC self-corrects	**M** misses the word, moves on
	T is told the word

								Notes
Mum	put	the	old	toys	in	the	car.	
The	children	were	sad.					
They	all	went	to	the	jumble	sale.		
The	children	wanted	to	buy	something.			
"What	a	lot	of	junk!"	said	Wilf.		
The	children	saw	their	toys.				
They	counted	their	money.					
It	was	time	to	go	home.			
"What's	in	the	bags?"	said	Mum.			
Oh	no!							

55 words long

Number of errors
(You'll need this in Step 4.)

To see an example of a completed oral reading record, go to page 28 in **Assess & Progress** *Teacher's Handbook: Stages 3–5.*

What next?
Now turn to Step 3: **Comprehension**

Reading Assessment   Step ❸

Child: .... Age: .... Class: ....

Teacher: .... Date: ....

The Jumble Sale

Stage 3
Book Band 3
Yellow

❸ Comprehension

KEY

C Complete
P Partial
N None
NE No evidence

Finish reading the book with the child. Have a reading conversation to find out how well they understood what they read (some example questions are provided below). Circle the letter that best reflects their understanding.

Retells story in own words   AF2   **Summarising**   C   P   N   NE

Example: Tell me about what happened in the book.

Retells story, *e.g. they take the old toys to the jumble sale; the children buy them back.*

Makes appropriate predictions   AF3   **Predicting**   C   P   N   NE

Example: Look at page 13. What do you think the children are going to buy?

Any sensible answer based on the book, *e.g. their old toys.*

Makes inferences about characters' feelings   AF3   **Clarifying**   C   P   N   NE

Example: How do you think Mum and Dad / the children feel about getting their old toys back?

Any sensible answer based on the book, *e.g. angry; cross; happy.*

Expresses personal opinion, giving reasoning   AF6   **Imagining**   C   P   N   NE

Example: What would you like to buy if you were at a jumble sale?

Shows opinion and explains their choice.

Activity:
Uses imagination to extend ideas from book   AF6   **Imagining**   C   P   N   NE

Example: Make a poster to advertise the jumble sale, telling people where / when it is and what there will be to buy (Activity Master 4 on page 103 of *Teacher's Handbook: Stages 3–5*).

Produces an informative advertisement.

To see an example of a reading conversation, go to page 29 in **Assess & Progress** *Teacher's Handbook: Stages 3–5.*

What next?

Now turn to Step 4: **Summary**

Reading Assessment Step 4

Oxford Reading Tree

ASSESS & PROGRESS

Child: .... Age: .... Class: ....

Teacher: .... Date: ....

4 Summary

Reading accuracy

Count the number of errors in the oral reading and circle the appropriate symbol.

KEY
- ● well developed
- ◖ developing
- ○ just beginning / not yet

●	0–3 errors	> 95%	**This book is likely to be appropriate, depending on comprehension.**
◖	4–6 errors	90–95%	
○	> 6 errors	< 90%	**This book is too hard.**

Reading strategies and skills

Shade each circle appropriately.

Reading fluency
- ○ Reading fluently
- ○ Using punctuation clues
- ○ Reading with expression
- ○ Doesn't insert or miss words

Establishing meaning
- ○ Knowing how to use a book
- ○ Predicting content
- ○ Making links between text and own experience
- ○ Using strategies to check meaning

Reading independently
- ○ Using appropriate strategies for reading unfamiliar words

Tick strategies observed for reading unfamiliar words

- ☐ Self-corrects for meaning
- ☐ 'Wrong' words make sense
- ☐ Uses phonics skills
- ☐ Makes connections with familiar words
- ☐ Uses picture clues

Reading performance *Review what you've observed during this assessment.*

Ask the child, "How do you think you did?"

....

Share with the child their reading strengths and targets for improvement.

Strengths: ....

Targets: ....

This assessment provides evidence towards National Curriculum level:

Towards	**1C**	1B
Level 1	**low**	secure

This book is appropriate for Level 1C. Mark where you think the child's reading level is, based on this assessment.

What next?

- ☐ Mostly ● — *Try Stage 4*
- ☐ Mostly ● and ◖ or mostly ◖ — *Ready for Stage 3*
- ☐ Mostly ○ — *Not yet ready for Stage 3*

*For next steps suggestions and activities, go to page 63 in **Assess & Progress** Teacher's Handbook: Stages 3–5.*

Reading Assessment   Step ❶

Child: .... Age: .... Class: ....

Teacher: .... Date: ....

The Big Match

Stage 3
Book Band 3
Yellow

The ducks play the foxes in a football match. Rick Duck and Max Fox both score goals. Max Fox kicks Rick Duck and gets sent off. Rick Duck scores another goal and the ducks win the match.

The 4-step assessment

❶ **Prior knowledge:** 2 minutes
what the child already knows about reading

❷ **Oral reading:** 8 minutes
what the child does when they read aloud

❸ **Comprehension:** 8 minutes
what the child understands when they read

❹ **Summary:** 2 minutes
outcomes and what to do next

❶ Prior knowledge

Give the child the book and discuss it together, before starting to read. Ask the questions below as part of the discussion.

1 What do you think this book is going to be about? How do you know?
Note any of the parts of the book the child uses to predict what it's about.

☐ Title   ☐ Cover   ☐ Pictures (inside the book)   ☐ Blurb   ☐ Scanning (flicking through)

☐ Other...

....

2 When you get stuck on a word, what do you do?
Note any of the strategies the child mentions.

☐ Sound it out   ☐ Re-read the sentence   ☐ Leave it out and read on

☐ Guess from the first letter   ☐ Look at the pictures   ☐ Break the word into syllables

☐ Ask for help   ☐ Other...

....

3 What do you do when you're reading and it doesn't make sense?
Note any of the strategies the child mentions.

☐ Read it again   ☐ Look at the pictures   ☐ Read on   ☐ Ask for help

☐ Other...

....

For more questions to help you find out about a child's knowledge of reading, to go page 64 in **Assess & Progress** *Teacher's Handbook: Stages 3–5.*

What next?
Now turn to Step 2: **Oral reading**

Reading Assessment Step ②

Child: .... Age: .... Class: ....

Teacher: .... Date: ....

② Oral reading

Ask the child to read to the end of page 5. Gradually withdraw support so that they read as independently as possible from page 6 to 13. (If the meaning is lost, ask them to pause, or give support.) In the table, mark any words you observe the child using a strategy to read, or that they read inaccurately, with the appropriate letters from the key. (You may want to summarise errors in the right-hand column, so you know how best to support the child in future.) At the end of the passage, record the number of errors.

KEY

Observed strategies	**Errors**
S sounds out / decodes	**( )** uses strategy with help *(record strategy in brackets)*
C uses context clues, e.g. pictures or meaning of the text as a whole	**W** reads the wrong word *(write substituted word)*
	M misses the word, moves on
SC self-corrects	**T** is told the word

							Notes
The	ref	rings	a	bell.	The	match	
has	begun!						
The	foxes	and	ducks	kick	the	ball.	
Rick	Duck	gets	the	ball	in.		
Max	Fox	gets	the	ball	in.		
The	ducks	get	the	ball.			
Max	Fox	kicks	Rick	Duck!			
The	duck	fans	quack.				
Get	him	off!					
The	ref	rings	his	bell.			
Get	off,	Max!					

53 words long

Number of errors

(You'll need this in Step 4.)

To see an example of a completed oral reading record, go to page 28 in **Assess & Progress** *Teacher's Handbook: Stages 3–5.*

What next?

Now turn to Step 3: **Comprehension**

Reading Assessment Step ③

Child: .... Age: .... Class: ....

Teacher: .... Date: ....

The Big Match

Stage 3
Book Band 3
Yellow

③ Comprehension

Finish reading the book with the child. Have a reading conversation to find out how well they understood what they read (some example questions are provided below). Circle the letter that best reflects their understanding.

KEY

C Complete
P Partial
N None
NE No evidence

Retells story in own words   AF2   Summarising   C   P   N   NE

Example: Tell me about what happened in the book.

Retells story, *e.g. the ducks and the foxes play football; the ducks win the match.*

Makes appropriate predictions   AF3   Predicting   C   P   N   NE

Example: Look at page 13. Which team do you think will win now? Why?

Any sensible answer based on the book, *e.g. the ducks because the foxes have fewer players.*

Makes inferences about characters' feelings   AF3   Imagining   C   P   N   NE

Example: How do you think the ducks and foxes feel at the end of the story?

Any sensible answer based on the book, *e.g. the ducks are happy because they won the match; the foxes are sad because they lost.*

Expresses personal opinion, giving reasoning   AF6   Imagining   C   P   N   NE

Example: If you were to join one of the teams for the next match, which would you join? Why?

Shows opinion and explains their choice.

Activity:
Uses imagination to extend ideas from book   AF6   Imagining   C   P   N   NE

Example: Design a certificate for the ducks' team for winning the match (Activity Master 5 on page 104 of *Teacher's Handbook: Stages 3–5*).

Produces certificate design including relevant information.

To see an example of a reading conversation, go to page 29 in **Assess & Progress** *Teacher's Handbook: Stages 3–5.*

What next?

Now turn to Step 4: **Summary**

Reading Assessment Step ④

Oxford Reading Tree

ASSESS & PROGRESS

Child: .... Age: .... Class: ....

Teacher: .... Date: ....

④ Summary

KEY

● well developed
◐ developing
○ just beginning / not yet

Reading accuracy

Count the number of errors in the oral reading and circle the appropriate symbol.

●	0 – 2 errors	> 95%	**This book is likely to be appropriate, depending on comprehension.**
◐	3 – 5 errors	90 – 95%	
○	> 5 errors	< 90%	**This book is too hard.**

Reading strategies and skills

Shade each circle appropriately.

Reading fluency
○ Reading fluently
○ Using punctuation clues
○ Reading with expression
○ Doesn't insert or miss words

Establishing meaning
○ Knowing how to use a book
○ Predicting content
○ Making links between text and own experience
○ Using strategies to check meaning

Reading independently
○ Using appropriate strategies for reading unfamiliar words

Tick strategies observed for reading unfamiliar words

☐ Self-corrects for meaning
☐ 'Wrong' words make sense
☐ Uses phonics skills
☐ Makes connections with familiar words
☐ Uses picture clues

Reading performance *Review what you've observed during this assessment.*

Ask the child, "How do you think you did?"

....

Share with the child their reading strengths and targets for improvement.

Strengths: ....

Targets: ....

This assessment provides evidence towards National Curriculum level:

Towards	**1C**	1B
Level 1	**low**	secure

This book is appropriate for Level 1C. Mark where you think the child's reading level is, based on this assessment.

What next?

☐ Mostly ● *Try Stage 4*

☐ Mostly ● and ◐ or mostly ◐ *Ready for Stage 3*

☐ Mostly ○ *Not yet ready for Stage 3*

*For next steps suggestions and activities, go to page 63 in **Assess & Progress** Teacher's Handbook: Stages 3–5.*

Reading Assessment Step **1**

Child: .... Age: .... Class: ....

Teacher: .... Date: ....

The Weather Vane

Stage 4
Book Band 4
Blue

Wilma and Wilf visit a building site with their Dad. A weather vane arrives at the site and the children jump over it. When the building is finished, the weather vane is fixed to the roof.
Biff doesn't believe that Wilf and Wilma have jumped over it … but Wilf has a photograph to prove it!

The 4-step assessment

1 Prior knowledge: 2 minutes
what the child already knows about reading

2 Oral reading: 8 minutes
what the child does when they read aloud

3 Comprehension: 8 minutes
what the child understands when they read

4 Summary: 2 minutes
outcomes and what to do next

1 Prior knowledge

Give the child the book and discuss it together, before starting to read. Ask the questions below as part of the discussion.

1 What do you think this book is going to be about? How do you know?
Note any of the parts of the book the child uses to predict what it's about.

☐ Title   ☐ Cover   ☐ Pictures (inside the book)   ☐ Blurb   ☐ Scanning (flicking through)

☐ Other..

....

2 When you get stuck on a word, what do you do?
Note any of the strategies the child mentions.

☐ Sound it out   ☐ Re-read the sentence   ☐ Leave it out and read on

☐ Guess from the first letter   ☐ Look at the pictures   ☐ Break the word into syllables

☐ Ask for help   ☐ Other..

....

3 What do you do when you're reading and it doesn't make sense?
Note any of the strategies the child mentions.

☐ Read it again   ☐ Look at the pictures   ☐ Read on   ☐ Ask for help

☐ Other..

....

*For more questions to help you find out about a child's knowledge of reading, go to page 64 in **Assess & Progress** Teacher's Handbook: Stages 3–5.*

What next?
Now turn to Step 2: **Oral reading**

Reading Assessment Step ❷

Oxford Reading Tree

ASSESS & PROGRESS

Child: .... Age: .... Class: ....

Teacher: .... Date: ....

❷ Oral reading

Ask the child to read to the end of page 5. Gradually withdraw support so that they read as independently as possible from page 6 to the end of the book. (If the meaning is lost, ask them to pause, or give support.) In the table, mark any words you observe the child using a strategy to read, or that they read inaccurately, with the appropriate letters from the key. (You may want to summarise errors in the right-hand column, so you know how best to support the child in future.) At the end of the passage, record the number of errors.

KEY

Observed strategies	**Errors**
S sounds out / decodes	**( )** uses strategy with help *(record strategy in brackets)*
C uses context clues, e.g. pictures or meaning of the text as a whole	**W** reads the wrong word *(write substituted word)*
SC self-corrects	**M** misses the word, moves on
	T is told the word

							Notes
Wilf	looked	at	the	weather	vane.		
Dad	had	an	idea.				
Wilf	jumped	over	the	weather	vane.		
"Be	careful,"	said	Dad.				
"Take	a	photograph	said	Wilma.			
She	jumped	over	the	weather	vane.		
The	weather	vane	went	on	the	roof.	
Wilf	took	a	photograph.				
"See	the	weather	vane,"	said	Wilf.		
"We've	jumped	over	it,"	said	Wilma.		
"What	a	tall	story!"	said	Biff.		
But	Wilf	had	a	photograph.			
"See,"	he	said.					

68 words long

Number of errors [ ]
(You'll need this in Step 4.)

To see an example of a completed oral reading record, go to page 28 in **Assess & Progress** *Teacher's Handbook: Stages 3–5.*

What next?
Now turn to Step 3: **Comprehension**

Reading Assessment Step ❸

Child: .... Age: .... Class: ....

Teacher: .... Date: ....

❸ Comprehension

Finish reading the book with the child. Have a reading conversation to find out how well they understood what they read (some example questions are provided below). Circle the letter that best reflects their understanding.

KEY

C Complete
P Partial
N None
NE No evidence

Retells story in own words AF2 Summarising C P N NE

Example: Tell me about what happened in the book.

Retells story, *e.g. the children go to the building site; Wilf and Wilma jump over the weather vane.*

Makes inferences about events and information AF3 Clarifying C P N NE

Example: Look at pages 2 and 3. How did Wilma speak to the man in the cab?

Any sensible answer based on the book, *e.g. on the radio.*

Makes appropriate predictions AF3 Predicting C P N NE

Example: Read pages 6 and 7. What do you think Dad's idea is?

Any sensible answer based on the book, *e.g. to put the weather vane on the roof.*

Makes inferences about characters' motivation AF6 Imagining C P N NE

Example: Read page 14. If you were Biff, would you believe Wilf and Wilma?

Shows ability to view the situation from another's point of view, *e.g. no, because it is on the roof.*

Activity:
Uses imagination to extend ideas from book AF6 Imagining C P N NE

Example: Write some safety rules for everyone who visits the building site. Look at what the characters are wearing on page 1 for ideas.

Produces a short list of sensible rules.

To see an example of a reading conversation, go to page 29 in **Assess & Progress** *Teacher's Handbook: Stages 3–5.*

What next?

Now turn to Step 4: **Summary**

Reading Assessment Step ❹

Oxford Reading Tree

ASSESS & PROGRESS

Child: .... Age: .... Class: ....

Teacher: .... Date: ....

❹ Summary

KEY

● well developed

◑ developing

○ just beginning / not yet

Reading accuracy

Count the number of errors in the oral reading and circle the appropriate symbol.

●	0–3 errors	> 95%	**This book is likely to be appropriate, depending on comprehension.**
◑	4–7 errors	90–95%	
○	> 7 errors	< 90%	**This book is too hard.**

Reading strategies and skills

Shade each circle appropriately.

Reading fluency
○ Reading fluently

○ Using punctuation clues

○ Reading with expression

○ Doesn't insert or miss words

Establishing meaning
○ Knowing how to use a book

○ Predicting content

○ Making links between text and own experience

○ Using strategies to check meaning

Reading independently
○ Using appropriate strategies for reading unfamiliar words

Tick strategies observed for reading unfamiliar words

☐ Self-corrects for meaning

☐ 'Wrong' words make sense

☐ Uses phonics skills

☐ Makes connections with familiar words

☐ Uses picture clues

Reading performance *Review what you've observed during this assessment.*

Ask the child, "How do you think you did?"

....

Share with the child their reading strengths and targets for improvement.

Strengths: ....

Targets: ....

This assessment provides evidence towards National Curriculum level:

1C	**1B**	1A
low	**secure**	high

This book is appropriate for Level 1B. Mark where you think the child's reading level is, based on this assessment.

What next?

☐ Mostly ● — *Try Stage 5*

☐ Mostly ● and ◑ or mostly ◑ — *Ready for Stage 4*

☐ Mostly ○ — *Not yet ready for Stage 4*

*For next steps suggestions and activities, go to page 63 in **Assess & Progress** Teacher's Handbook: Stages 3–5.*

Reading Assessment Step **1**

Child: .... Age: .... Class: ....

Teacher: .... Date: ....

Queen Anneena's Feast

Stage 4
Book Band 4
Blue

Queen Anneena has invited fifteen queens to her feast. All the queens eat different things, but Queen Teeny Weeny will only eat one green leaf!

The 4-step assessment

1 **Prior knowledge:** 2 minutes
what the child already knows about reading

2 **Oral reading:** 8 minutes
what the child does when they read aloud

3 **Comprehension:** 8 minutes
what the child understands when they read

4 **Summary:** 2 minutes
outcomes and what to do next

1 Prior knowledge

Give the child the book and discuss it together, before starting to read. Ask the questions below as part of the discussion.

1 What do you think this book is going to be about? How do you know?
Note any of the parts of the book the child uses to predict what it's about.

☐ Title   ☐ Cover   ☐ Pictures (inside the book)   ☐ Blurb   ☐ Scanning (flicking through)

☐ Other..

....

2 When you get stuck on a word, what do you do?
Note any of the strategies the child mentions.

☐ Sound it out   ☐ Re-read the sentence   ☐ Leave it out and read on

☐ Guess from the first letter   ☐ Look at the pictures   ☐ Break the word into syllables

☐ Ask for help   ☐ Other...

....

3 What do you do when you're reading and it doesn't make sense?
Note any of the strategies the child mentions.

☐ Read it again   ☐ Look at the pictures   ☐ Read on   ☐ Ask for help

☐ Other..

....

For more questions to help you find out about a child's knowledge of reading, go to page 64 in **Assess & Progress** *Teacher's Handbook: Stages 3–5.*

What next?
Now turn to Step 2: **Oral reading**

Reading Assessment Step ❷

Oxford Reading Tree

ASSESS & PROGRESS

Child: .... Age: .... Class: ....

Teacher: .... Date: ....

❷ Oral reading

Ask the child to read to the end of page 5. Gradually withdraw support so that they read as independently as possible from page 6 to 11. (If the meaning is lost, ask them to pause, or give support.) In the table, mark any words you observe the child using a strategy to read, or that they read inaccurately, with the appropriate letters from the key. (You may want to summarise errors in the right-hand column, so you know how best to support the child in future.) At the end of the passage, record the number of errors.

KEY

Observed strategies

S sounds out / decodes
C uses context clues, e.g. pictures or meaning of the text as a whole
SC self-corrects

Errors

( ) uses strategy with help *(record strategy in brackets)*
W reads the wrong word *(write substituted word)*
M misses the word, moves on
T is told the word

							Notes
"Have	some	peas	and	beans,"	said		
Queen	Jean.						
"No,"	said	Queen	Teeny	Weeny.			
"Have	some	jelly	and	cream,"	said		
Queen	Nelly.						
"No,"	said	Queen	Teeny	Weeny.			
"What	do	you	want	to	eat	then?"	
said	Queen	Anneena.					
"One	green	leaf,"	said				
Queen	Teeny	Weeny.	But	there			
was	not	a	leaf	to	be	seen!	

52 words long

Number of errors
(You'll need this in Step 4.)

To see an example of a completed oral reading record, go to page 28 in **Assess & Progress** *Teacher's Handbook: Stages 3–5.*

What next?
Now turn to Step 3: **Comprehension**

Reading Assessment   Step ❸

Child: .... Age: .... Class: ....

Teacher: .... Date: ....

Queen Anneena's Feast

Stage 4
Book Band 4
Blue

❸ Comprehension

Finish reading the book with the child. Have a reading conversation to find out how well they understood what they read (some example questions are provided below). Circle the letter that best reflects their understanding.

KEY

C Complete
P Partial
N None
NE No evidence

Retells story in own words   AF2   Summarising   C   P   N   NE

Example: Tell me about what happened in the book.

Retells story, *e.g. Queen Anneena has a feast; Queen Teeny Weeny will only eat a leaf.*

Makes appropriate predictions   AF3   Predicting   C   P   N   NE

Example: If Queen Teeny Weeny were offered some chocolate to eat, do you think she would have eaten it? Why/why not?

Any sensible answer based on the book, *e.g. no, she would only eat a leaf.*

Makes inferences about reasons for actions   AF3   Clarifying   C   P   N   NE

Example: What did Queen Teeny Weeny do at the end of the story? Why do you think she did this?

Any sensible answer based on the book, *e.g. she went home to clean her teeth because she had just eaten.*

Expresses personal opinion, giving reasoning   AF6   Imagining   C   P   N   NE

Example: What would you like to eat at a feast? Would you be happy with a leaf?

Shows opinion and explains their answer.

Activity:
Uses imagination to extend ideas from book   AF6   Imagining   C   P   N   NE

Example: Imagine you are Queen Anneena. Write an invitation to your feast. Think about what information you will need to include (Activity Master 6 on page 105 of *Teacher's Handbook: Stages 3–5*).

Produces invitation including relevant information.

To see an example of a reading conversation, go to page 29 in **Assess & Progress** *Teacher's Handbook: Stages 3–5.*

What next?
Now turn to Step 4: **Summary**

<table>
<tr><td>

Queen Anneena's Feast

Stage 4
Book Band 4
Blue

</td><td>

Reading Assessment   Step ④

Child: .... Age: .... Class: ....

Teacher: .... Date: ....

</td><td>

</td></tr>
</table>

④ Summary

Reading accuracy

Count the number of errors in the oral reading and circle the appropriate symbol.

●	0 – 3 errors	> 95%	This book is likely to be appropriate, depending on comprehension.
◑	4 – 5 errors	90 – 95%	
○	> 5 errors	< 90%	This book is too hard.

KEY
- ● well developed
- ◑ developing
- ○ just beginning / not yet

Reading strategies and skills

Shade each circle appropriately.

Reading fluency
- ○ Reading fluently
- ○ Using punctuation clues
- ○ Reading with expression
- ○ Doesn't insert or miss words

Establishing meaning
- ○ Knowing how to use a book
- ○ Predicting content
- ○ Making links between text and own experience
- ○ Using strategies to check meaning

Reading independently
- ○ Using appropriate strategies for reading unfamiliar words

Tick strategies observed for reading unfamiliar words

- ☐ Self-corrects for meaning
- ☐ 'Wrong' words make sense
- ☐ Uses phonics skills
- ☐ Makes connections with familiar words
- ☐ Uses picture clues

Reading performance   *Review what you've observed during this assessment.*

Ask the child, "How do you think you did?"

....

Share with the child their reading strengths and targets for improvement.

Strengths: ....

Targets: ....

This assessment provides evidence towards National Curriculum level:

1C	**1B**	1A
low	**secure**	high

This book is appropriate for Level 1B. Mark where you think the child's reading level is, based on this assessment.

What next?
- ☐ Mostly ●   *Try Stage 5*
- ☐ Mostly ● and ◑ or mostly ◑   *Ready for Stage 4*
- ☐ Mostly ○   *Not yet ready for Stage 4*

*For next steps suggestions and activities, go to page 63 in **Assess & Progress** Teacher's Handbook: Stages 3–5.*

Reading Assessment Step **1**

Child: .... Age: .... Class: ....

Teacher: .... Date: ....

The New Baby

Stage 5
Book Band 5
Green

Jo is expecting a baby. Everyone tries to find old baby things for her. At school, the children learn about babies. When Jo's baby is born, Kipper thinks she is great – but doesn't want to help change her nappy!

The 4-step assessment

1 **Prior knowledge:**   2 minutes
what the child already knows about reading

2 **Oral reading:**   8 minutes
what the child does when they read aloud

3 **Comprehension:**   8 minutes
what the child understands when they read

4 **Summary:**   2 minutes
outcomes and what to do next

1 Prior knowledge

Give the child the book and discuss it together, before starting to read. Ask the questions below as part of the discussion.

1 What do you think this book is going to be about? How do you know?

Note any of the parts of the book the child uses to predict what it's about.

☐ Title   ☐ Cover   ☐ Pictures (inside the book)   ☐ Blurb   ☐ Scanning (flicking through)

☐ Other...

2 When you get stuck on a word, what do you do?

Note any of the strategies the child mentions.

☐ Sound it out   ☐ Re-read the sentence   ☐ Leave it out and read on

☐ Guess from the first letter   ☐ Look at the pictures   ☐ Break the word into syllables

☐ Ask for help   ☐ Other ....

3 What do you do when you're reading and it doesn't make sense?

Note any of the strategies the child mentions.

☐ Read it again   ☐ Look at the pictures   ☐ Read on   ☐ Ask for help

☐ Other...

For more questions to help you find out about a child's knowledge of reading, go to page 64 in **Assess & Progress** *Teacher's Handbook: Stages 3–5.*

What next?

Now turn to Step 2: **Oral reading**

Reading Assessment Step ❷

Child: .... Age: .... Class: ....

Teacher: .... Date: ....

❷ Oral reading

Ask the child to read to the end of page 3. Gradually withdraw support so that they read as independently as possible from page 4 to 8. (If the meaning is lost, ask them to pause, or give support.) In the table, mark any words you observe the child using a strategy to read, or that they read inaccurately, with the appropriate letters from the key. (You may want to summarise errors in the right-hand column, so you know how best to support the child in future.) At the end of the passage, record the number of errors.

KEY

Observed strategies	Errors
S sounds out / decodes	**( )** uses strategy with help *(record strategy in brackets)*
C uses context clues, e.g. pictures or meaning of the text as a whole	**W** reads the wrong word *(write substituted word)*
SC self-corrects	**M** misses the word, moves on
	T is told the word

							Notes
Wilma	told	Biff	and	Chip.			
"Jo	is	expecting	a	baby,"	she	said.	
"What	good	news!"	said	Chip.			
Biff	and	Chip	went	home.			
"Jo	is	expecting	a	baby,"	said	Chip.	
"What	good	news!"	said	Mum.			
Dad	found	the	old	cot.			
"Oh	look!"	said	Mum.	"Kipper	had	it	
when	he	was	a	baby."			
The	cot	looked	a	bit	scruffy.		
It	needed	a	new	mattress.			
"We	can	do	it	up,"	said	Dad.	
Biff	and	Chip	told	Kipper.			
"Jo	is	expecting	a	baby,"	they	said.	
"That's	brilliant!"	said	Kipper.				

85 words long

Number of errors
(You'll need this in Step 4.)

To see an example of a reading conversation, go to page 28 in **Assess & Progress** *Teacher's Handbook: Stages 3–5.*

What next?
Now turn to Step 3: **Comprehension**

Reading Assessment Step ❸

Child:	Age: .... Class: ....
Teacher:	Date: ....

The New Baby

Stage 5
Book Band 5
Green

❸ Comprehension

Finish reading the book with the child. Have a reading conversation to find out how well they understood what they read (some example questions are provided below). Circle the letter that best reflects their understanding.

KEY

C Complete
P Partial
N None
NE No evidence

Retells story in own words AF2 Summarising   **C   P   N   NE**

Example: Tell me about what happened in the book.

Retells story, *e.g. Jo has a baby; everyone is excited.*

Makes inferences about reasons AF3 Imagining   **C   P   N   NE**

Example: Why did Wilf make a big chart?

Any sensible answer based on the book, *e.g. to guess how much the baby will weigh.*

Makes inferences about events and information AF3 Clarifying   **C   P   N   NE**

Example: Why do you think Kipper didn't want to help at the end of the story?

Any sensible answer based on the book, *e.g. Vicky's nappy was dirty/smelly.*

Uses imagination to think of relevant questions AF6 Questioning   **C   P   N   NE**

Example: If you could ask Miss Green a question about babies, what would you ask?

Any sensible question about babies, *e.g. how do you hold a baby?*

Activity:
Makes inferences about characters' feelings AF3 Imagining   **C   P   N   NE**

Example: Look at page 21. Draw and fill in a thought bubble for Jo, and another one for Wilma.

Any sensible thoughts based on the book, *e.g. Jo: "I'm so pleased I've had my baby!"*

To see an example of a reading conversation, go to
page 29 in **Assess & Progress** *Teacher's Handbook: Stages 3–5.*

What next?
Now turn to Step 4: **Summary**

Reading Assessment Step ❹

Oxford Reading Tree

ASSESS & PROGRESS

Child: .... Age: .... Class: ....

Teacher: .... Date: ....

❹ Summary

KEY

● well developed

◑ developing

○ just beginning / not yet

Reading accuracy

Count the number of errors in the oral reading and circle the appropriate symbol.

●	0 – 4 errors	> 95%	This book is likely to be appropriate, depending on comprehension.
◑	5 – 9 errors	90 – 95%	
○	> 9 errors	< 90%	This book is too hard.

Reading strategies and skills

Shade each circle appropriately.

Reading fluency
○ Reading fluently
○ Using punctuation clues
○ Reading with expression
○ Doesn't insert or miss words

Establishing meaning
○ Knowing how to use a book
○ Predicting content
○ Making links between text and own experience
○ Using strategies to check meaning

Reading independently
○ Using appropriate strategies for reading unfamiliar words

Tick strategies observed for reading unfamiliar words

☐ Self-corrects for meaning
☐ 'Wrong' words make sense
☐ Uses phonics skills

☐ Makes connections with familiar words
☐ Uses picture clues

Reading performance *Review what you've observed during this assessment.*

Ask the child, "How do you think you did?"

....

Share with the child their reading strengths and targets for improvement.

Strengths: ....

Targets: ....

This assessment provides evidence towards National Curriculum level:

1B	**1A**	2C
secure	**high**	low

This book is appropriate for Level 1A. Mark where you think the child's reading level is, based on this assessment.

What next?

☐ Mostly ● *Try Stage 6*

☐ Mostly ● and ◑ or mostly ◑ *Ready for Stage 5*

☐ Mostly ○ *Not yet ready for Stage 5*

*For next steps suggestions and activities, go to page 63 in **Assess & Progress** Teacher's Handbook: Stages 3–5.*

Reading Assessment Step ❶

Child: .... Age: .... Class: ....

Teacher: .... Date: ....

Sue Kangaroo

Stage 5
Book Band 5
Green

It's Sue's first day at school. She has fun painting, gluing and playing the spoons. She is upset she can't take the things home with her, but very happy when she learns there's school tomorrow, too!

The 4-step assessment

❶ **Prior knowledge:**   2 minutes
what the child already knows about reading

❷ **Oral reading:**   8 minutes
what the child does when they read aloud

❸ **Comprehension:**   8 minutes
what the child understands when they read

❹ **Summary:**   2 minutes
outcomes and what to do next

❶ Prior knowledge

Give the child the book and discuss it together, before starting to read. Ask the questions below as part of the discussion.

1 What do you think this book is going to be about? How do you know?
Note any of the parts of the book the child uses to predict what it's about.

☐ Title   ☐ Cover   ☐ Pictures (inside the book)   ☐ Blurb   ☐ Scanning (flicking through)

☐ Other..

2 When you get stuck on a word, what do you do?
Note any of the strategies the child mentions.

☐ Sound it out   ☐ Re-read the sentence   ☐ Leave it out and read on

☐ Guess from the first letter   ☐ Look at the pictures   ☐ Break the word into syllables

☐ Ask for help   ☐ Other...

3 What do you do when you're reading and it doesn't make sense?
Note any of the strategies the child mentions.

☐ Read it again   ☐ Look at the pictures   ☐ Read on   ☐ Ask for help

☐ Other..

For more questions to help you find out about a child's knowledge of reading, go to page 64 in **Assess & Progress** *Teacher's Handbook: Stages 3–5.*

What next?
Now turn to Step 2: **Oral reading**

Reading Assessment Step ❷

Child: .... Age: .... Class: ....

Teacher: .... Date: ....

Oxford Reading Tree

ASSESS & PROGRESS

❷ Oral reading

Ask the child to read to the end of page 5. Gradually withdraw support so that they read as independently as possible from page 6 to 14. (If the meaning is lost, ask them to pause, or give support.) In the table, mark any words you observe the child using a strategy to read, or that they read inaccurately, with the appropriate letters from the key. (You may want to summarise errors in the right-hand column, so you know how best to support the child in future.) At the end of the passage, record the number of errors.

KEY

Observed strategies	Errors
S sounds out / decodes	**( )** uses strategy with help *(record strategy in brackets)*
C uses context clues, e.g. pictures or meaning of the text as a whole	**W** reads the wrong word *(write substituted word)*
SC self-corrects	**M** misses the word, moves on
	T is told the word

							Notes
"Time	to	paint,"	says	Mrs	Drew.		
Sue	says,	"I	like	red	and	blue."	
"Time	to	glue,"	says	Mrs	Drew.		
"Sue	can	glue	a	kangaroo!"			
"Dinner	time,"	says	Mrs	Drew.			
"This	is	yummy	stew,"	says	Sue.		
"Music	time,"	says	Mrs	Drew.			
"I	can	play	the	spoons!"	says	Sue.	
"Home	time	soon,"	says	Mrs	Drew.		

53 words long

Number of errors

(You'll need this in Step 4.)

To see an example of a completed oral reading record, go to page 28 in **Assess & Progress** *Teacher's Handbook: Stages 3–5.*

What next?

Now turn to Step 3: **Comprehension**

Reading Assessment   Step ❸

Child: ....   Age: .... Class: ....

Teacher: ....   Date: ....

Sue Kangaroo

Stage 5
Book Band 5
Green

❸ Comprehension

Finish reading the book with the child. Have a reading conversation to find out how well they understood what they read (some example questions are provided below). Circle the letter that best reflects their understanding.

KEY

C Complete
P Partial
N None
NE No evidence

Retells story in own words   AF2   Summarising   C   P   N   NE

Example: Tell me about what happened in the book.

Retells story, *e.g. Sue went to school; she thought it was cool.*

Makes inferences about characters' motivations   AF3   Clarifying   C   P   N   NE

Example: Look at page 19. Why do you think Sue wanted to take the things home with her?

Any sensible answer based on the book, *e.g. because she wanted to play with them at home too.*

Makes inferences about characters' feelings   AF3   Clarifying   C   P   N   NE

Example: Did Sue like school in the end? Do you think she will want to go again tomorrow?

Any sensible answer based on the book, *e.g. yes, she was happy there was school tomorrow; she said "school is cool!"*

Expresses personal opinion, giving reasoning for response   AF6   Imagining   C   P   N   NE

Example: Think about the things that Sue did in school. Which would you most enjoy? Why?

Shows opinion and explains their choice, *e.g. painting, because I like bright colours.*

Activity:
Uses imagination to extend ideas from book   AF6   Imagining   C   P   N   NE

Example: Write a short plan of what Sue will do in school tomorrow.

Produces brief list of school activities.

To see an example of a reading conversation, go to page 29 in **Assess & Progress** *Teacher's Handbook: Stages 3–5.*

What next?

Now turn to Step 4: **Summary**

<table>
<tr><td>

Sue Kangaroo

Stage 5
Book Band 5
Green

</td><td>

Reading Assessment Step 4

Child: .... Age: .... Class: ....

Teacher: .... Date: ....

</td><td>

Oxford Reading Tree

ASSESS & PROGRESS

</td></tr>
</table>

4 Summary

Reading accuracy

Count the number of errors in the oral reading and circle the appropriate symbol.

●	0 – 3 errors	> 95%	**This book is likely to be appropriate, depending on comprehension.**
◐	4 – 5 errors	90 – 95%	
○	> 5 errors	< 90%	**This book is too hard.**

Reading strategies and skills

Shade each circle appropriately.

Reading fluency
- ○ Reading fluently
- ○ Using punctuation clues
- ○ Reading with expression
- ○ Doesn't insert or miss words

Establishing meaning
- ○ Knowing how to use a book
- ○ Predicting content
- ○ Making links between text and own experience
- ○ Using strategies to check meaning

Reading independently
- ○ Using appropriate strategies for reading unfamiliar words

Tick strategies observed for reading unfamiliar words

- ☐ Self-corrects for meaning
- ☐ 'Wrong' words make sense
- ☐ Uses phonics skills
- ☐ Makes connections with familiar words
- ☐ Uses picture clues

Reading performance *Review what you've observed during this assessment.*

Ask the child, "How do you think you did?"

....

Share with the child their reading strengths and targets for improvement.

Strengths: ....

Targets: ....

<table>
<tr><td>

This assessment provides evidence towards National Curriculum level:

1B	**1A**	2C
secure	**high**	low

This book is appropriate for Level 1A. Mark where you think the child's reading level is, based on this assessment.

</td><td>

What next?

- ☐ Mostly ● — *Try Stage 6*
- ☐ Mostly ● and ◐ or mostly ◐ — *Ready for Stage 5*
- ☐ Mostly ○ — *Not yet ready for Stage 5*

</td></tr>
</table>

*For next steps suggestions and activities, go to page 63 in **Assess & Progress** Teacher's Handbook: Stages 3–5.*

What next?

Find out more

After carrying out a Benchmark Book Reading Assessment, you may want to investigate further to double-check the outcome, gather more evidence, or pinpoint problems more exactly. Resources to help you do this are in the next section, **Find out more**, on pages 64–77. This section provides:

- example questions to help you find out about a child's general reading attitudes and behaviours – page 64
- guidance on how to use the miscue analysis (Step 2 of the Reading Assessment) to find out more about the strategies children are using and mistakes they are making – pages 65–66
- guidance and assessment sheets for using the Unseen Text cards to reassess aspects of reading – pages 67–74
- phonics checklists to enable you to focus specifically on phonics skills – pages 75–77

Problems and solutions

If a Reading Assessment or further investigation reveals that a child has a weakness in a particular area, the **Problems and solutions** section on pages 78–90 provides ideas and activities to help get their reading back on track.

Find out more

Reading attitudes and experience

If a child's reading progress is not matching your expectations, try finding out more about their reading experiences and how they see themselves as readers. These insights into a child's reading world can be very informative. Some example questions to help you find out more about children as readers are given below. Keep notes to see whether their answers change over time, or to share with colleagues.

Attitudes to reading

- Do you like listening to stories at school and at home?
- Do you like reading stories yourself? What kinds of stories?
- Do you think you are good at reading?
- What kinds of things do you get stuck on when you're reading? What do you do when you're stuck at school? What about when you're at home?
- Would you like to be even better at reading? What would help you to get even better? What should we do?

Exposure to texts and stories

- Does your [carer] read stories to you? What kinds of stories do you like?
- Do you listen to story CDs or watch DVDs of stories? Who are the characters / people in the stories?

Models for reading

- Who reads in your house? What do you see them reading?
- Do you have newspapers in your house? Who reads them?

Access to reading

- Do you have any books of your own or to share with your brother/ sister? What kinds of books are they?
- Do you get any comics or magazines? What are they called?
- Do you borrow books from the library?

Experience of reading at home

- Do you read to your [carer] at home? When do you read to them?
- Do you read to yourself at home? Where do you like reading? What kinds of books do you read?
- Do you read books that don't come from school? Where do they come from? Do you choose them yourself?

Learning from a miscue analysis

Step 2 of the Benchmark Book Reading Assessment involves completing a miscue analysis to find the number of errors in a child's reading. You can use the same analysis to find out more. Use the Notes column (on the right-hand side) to summarize the kinds of strategies and errors that came up, and check the text to see which words posed problems. The results can be very revealing.

Mostly S (sounding out or decoding)

If a child often makes mistakes in sounding out words, you know that they need to develop their phonics knowledge and skills. The phonics checklists (pages 75–77) help you find out more about which phonics skills the child is confident using, and which they need more support or practice with. The **Problems and solutions** section (pages 78–90) then gives further support and activity ideas.

Mostly C (using context clues)

Research suggests that children need a working knowledge of phonics to support their reading. If a child is relying heavily on context clues and many of their errors seem to result from this, try asking them to read an Unseen Text (pages 68–74). This is a short text with no pictures, written especially for *Assess & Progress*. It will show how well the child can read and understand text without support from pictures.

Mostly W (reading the wrong word or substituting words)

If a child often reads the wrong word, look carefully both at the word they misread and at the word they substitute. If you need to, use an Unseen Text (pages 68–74) to confirm the pattern of errors.

Are the misread words 'tricky' or phonically regular?
If the misread words are phonically regular, find out more about the child's level of phonic knowledge and skill using the phonics checklists (pages 75–77).

Are the substitute words visually similar to the correct words (e.g. of instead of for, can instead of come) or do they have a similar meaning (e.g. wood instead of forest)?

If they're similar in meaning, look very closely at how the child is reading: how much attention are they paying to the words, and how much to the context? Good readers use meaning and context to confirm they have read correctly, but if a child is using context and making errors, they're probably relying too much on context, and not enough on decoding. To assess their ability to decode, ask them to read an Unseen Text (pages 68–74), or use the phonics checklists (pages 75–77).

Mostly M (missing out words)

If a child is missing out words (or reading them inaudibly) and moving on, they may be focusing on reading words rather than making meaning. Consider trying some easier books to allow them to concentrate on making meaning.

Mostly T (being told the correct word)

If there are a lot of words a child just can't read, the book may be too difficult, they may lack confidence, or they may be waiting for help. From your knowledge of the child's reading, think about whether you'd expect them to make this type of error. It may help to explore how the child feels about themselves as a reader and their experiences of reading (see page 64).

Using an Unseen Text

An Unseen Text card helps you to confirm the result of a Reading Assessment or to focus on one aspect of a child's reading. As each Unseen Text is short and has no pictures, it enables you to find out how accurately a child can read and how effectively they make meaning.

Use an Unseen Text to find out whether a child can:
- recognize sounds from their written representations (that is, recognize grapheme-phoneme correspondences)
- blend sounds effectively to read words, including longer words
- recognize high frequency words, including tricky (non-decodable) words
- use their phonic knowledge and understanding of context to work out new tricky words
- read for meaning as well as decoding effectively
- read and understand text without relying on pictures for support.

Assess & Progress provides one Unseen Text card for each Oxford Reading Tree Stage from 1+ to 11. Each Unseen Text is carefully levelled to indicate the expected knowledge of phonics and high frequency words, and for comprehension.

Title	Stage	Book Band*	Genre	Length
Pat and Pam	1+	1: Pink	Fiction	15 words
The Duck and the Hen	2	2: Red	Fiction	30 words
At the Shops	3	3: Yellow	Non-fiction	78 words
On the Farm	4	4: Blue	Non-fiction	104 words
My Trip to the Beach	5	5: Green	Fiction	105 words
How to Keep Healthy	6	6: Orange	Non-fiction	104 words
The Great Fire of London	7	7: Turquoise	Non-fiction	105 words
Sheema's Big Day	8	8: Purple	Fiction	121 words
Animals Around the World	9	9: Gold	Non-fiction	106 words
One Dark Night	10	10: White	Fiction	123 words
Volcanoes	11	11: Lime	Non-fiction	121 words

*** Best fit**

Photocopiable Oral Reading (miscue analysis) and Comprehension
Assessments for the Stages 3–5 Unseen Texts are provided on pages
69–74. These give you the option of carrying out a mini Reading
Assessment with the Unseen Text.

Note that if a child's reading comprehension is significantly
better than their reading accuracy, this can be associated with
specific learning difficulties (including dyslexia). If a mini Reading
Assessment results in a poor oral reading result compared to
the level of comprehension, consider checking with your special
needs teacher.

Unseen Text Assessment

Child: .... **Age:** .... **Class:** ....

Teacher: .... **Date:** ....

Oral reading

Ask the child to read the Unseen Text card. Allow them to read it as independently as possible. (If the meaning is lost, ask them to pause, or give support.) In the table, mark any words you observe the child using a strategy to read, or that they read inaccurately, with the appropriate letters from the key. (You may want to summarise errors in the right-hand column, so you know how best to support the child in future.) At the end of the passage, record the number of errors.

KEY

Observed strategies

S sounds out / decodes

C uses context clues, e.g. pictures or meaning of the text as a whole

SC self-corrects

Errors

( ) uses strategy with help *(record strategy in brackets)*

W reads the wrong word *(write substituted word)*

M misses the word, moves on

T is told the word

										Notes
Mum	needs	a	coat.	We	go					
to	the	shop	up	the	road.					
Mum	looks	at	all	the	coats,					
but	they	are	too	long	for	her.				
Mum	sees	a	cool	coat,	but					
it	is	too	tight.							
Mum	and	I	go	down	the	road				
to	the	pet	shop.	We	need	to				
get	food	for	the	fish.	I	see	a	lot		
of	chicks	and	a	rat	with					
a	long	tail.								
"Mum!"	I	yell.	"Can	we	get					
this	rat?"									
"No!"	yells	Mum.								

78 words long

Number of errors [ ]

●	0 – 4 errors	> 95%	**This text is likely to be appropriate, depending on comprehension.**
◐	5 – 8 errors	90 – 95%	
○	> 8 errors	< 90%	**This text is too hard.**

To see an example of a completed oral reading record, go to page 28 in **Assess & Progress** Teacher's Handbook: Stages 3–5.

What next?

Now go to page 70: **Comprehension.**

Unseen Text Assessment

Child: .... Age: .... Class: ....

Teacher: .... Date: ....

Comprehension

Finish reading the text with the child. Have a reading conversation to find out how well they understood what they read (some example questions are provided below). Circle the letter that best reflects their understanding.

KEY

C Complete
P Partial
N None
NE No evidence

Retells story in own words   AF2   Summarising   C   P   N   NE

Example: Can you tell me what happened in the story?

Retells story, *e.g. The person in the story goes to the shops with their mum.*

Retells information in own words   AF2   Summarising   C   P   N   NE

Example: What did Mum need?

Any sensible answer based on the text, *e.g. She needed a new coat.*

Retells information in own words   AF2   Summarising   C   P   N   NE

Example: Why didn't she get the cool coat?

Any sensible answer based on the text, *e.g. because it was too small for her.*

Makes inferences about reasons   AF3   Clarifying   C   P   N   NE

Example: Why do you think Mum yelled "No!"?

Any sensible answer, *e.g. because she doesn't like rats.*

Makes inferences about events and ideas   AF3   Imagining   C   P   N   NE

Example: Why do you think Mum needed a new coat?

Any sensible answer, *e.g. her old one was worn out; she was going somewhere special.*

To see an example of a reading conversation, go to page 29
in **Assess & Progress** *Teacher's Handbook: Stages 3–5.*

Oxford Reading Tree — ASSESS & PROGRESS

Unseen Text Assessment

On the Farm

Stage 4
Book Band 4
Blue

Child: .... Age: .... Class: ....

Teacher: .... Date: ....

Oral reading

Ask the child to read the Unseen Text card. Allow them to read it as independently as possible. (If the meaning is lost, ask them to pause, or give support.) In the table, mark any words you observe the child using a strategy to read, or that they read inaccurately, with the appropriate letters from the key. (You may want to summarise errors in the right-hand column, so you know how best to support the child in future.) At the end of the passage, record the number of errors.

KEY

Observed strategies	Errors
S sounds out / decodes	**( )** uses strategy with help *(record strategy in brackets)*
C uses context clues, e.g. pictures or meaning of the text as a whole	**W** reads the wrong word *(write substituted word)*
SC self-corrects	**M** misses the word, moves on
	T is told the word

								Notes
The	farmer	has	a	lot	of	jobs		
to	do.	She	has	to	feed	the	chickens.	
They	peck	at	the	grain	with	their		
beaks.	Then	she	has	to	go	to		
the	barn.	She	feeds	the	cows	and		
the	sheep.	She	lifts	up	the	cows'	feet	
to	check	them.						
Next,	she	checks	the	little	goat.			
Its	pen	is	near	the	barn.	The	pigs	
are	near	the	barn	too.	One	pig		
is	digging	up	the	soft	mud	in		
the	pen.	The	farmer	feeds	them	with		
grain	too.	They	eat	it	all	up.		
Soon	the	farmer	will	go	back			
to	the	farm.	Then	she	will	feed		
her	children.							

104 words long

Number of errors

●	0–5 errors	> 95%	**This text is likely to be appropriate, depending on comprehension.**
◑	6–10 errors	90–95%	
○	> 10 errors	< 90%	**This text is too hard.**

To see an example of a completed oral reading record, go to page 28 in **Assess & Progress** *Teacher's Handbook: Stages 3–5.*

What next?

Now go to page 72: **Comprehension.**

Unseen Text Assessment

Child: .... Age: .... Class: ....

Teacher: .... Date: ....

Comprehension

Finish reading the text with the child. Have a reading conversation to find out how well they understood what they read (some example questions are provided below). Circle the letter that best reflects their understanding.

KEY

C Complete
P Partial
N None
NE No evidence

Retells information in own words AF2 Summarising   C   P   N   NE

Example: What does the farmer do first in the morning?

Retells information, *e.g. she feeds the chickens.*

Retells information in own words AF2 Summarising   C   P   N   NE

Example: Where does the little goat live?

Retells information, *e.g. near the barn, near the pigs.*

Makes deductions about events and information AF3 Clarifying   C   P   N   NE

Example: Is the farmer a man or a woman? How do you know?

A woman; provides reasoning for this choice, *e.g. it says 'she', not 'he'.*

Makes inferences about characters' feelings AF3 Imagining   C   P   N   NE

Example: How do you think the farmer feels when she gets back home? Why?

Any sensible answer based on the book, *e.g. tired;* provides reasoning, *e.g. from all that work.*

Makes appropriate predictions AF3 Predicting   C   P   N   NE

Example: What do you think she will do first when she gets back home?

Any sensible predictions based on the book, *e.g. wash her hands; put the kettle on; start breakfast.*

---

*To see an example of a reading conversation, go to page 29
in* **Assess & Progress** *Teacher's Handbook: Stages 3–5.*

© *Oxford University Press 2009   This page can be copied for use in the purchasing school.*

Unseen Text Assessment

My Trip to the Beach

Stage 5
Book Band 5
Green

Child: .... Age: .... Class: ....

Teacher: .... Date: ....

Oral reading

Ask the child to read the Unseen Text card. Allow them to read it as independently as possible. (If the meaning is lost, ask them to pause, or give support.) In the table, mark any words you observe the child using a strategy to read, or that they read inaccurately, with the appropriate letters from the key. (You may want to summarise errors in the right-hand column, so you know how best to support the child in future.) At the end of the passage, record the number of errors.

KEY

Observed strategies	Errors
S sounds out / decodes	**( )** uses strategy with help *(record strategy in brackets)*
C uses context clues, e.g. pictures or meaning of the text as a whole	**W** reads the wrong word *(write substituted word)*
SC self-corrects	**M** misses the word, moves on
	T is told the word

										Notes
Last	week	we	went	to	the	beach.				
I	was	kicking	my	ball	about	and				
Ben	ran	to	get	it.						
There	was	a	shiny	thing	next	to				
the	ball,	in	the	sand.	He	gave				
a	shout.	"Look	at	this!"						
I	went	to	have	a	look.	I	could	see		
a	point	sticking	out	of	the	sand.				
What	was	under	the	sand?						
We	began	digging.	Lots	of	people					
came	to	see.	Their	feet	got	in				
the	way	but	we	kept	on	digging.				
At	last	we	could	see	what	it				
was –	a	chest.	We	took	off	the	lid.			
The	people	let	out	a	gasp.	We	had			
found	a	crown!								

105 words long

Number of errors [ ]

●	0 – 5 errors	> 95%	This text is likely to be appropriate, depending on comprehension.
◐	6 – 11 errors	90 – 95%	
○	> 11 errors	< 90%	This text is too hard.

To see an example of a completed oral reading record, go to page 28 in **Assess & Progress** *Teacher's Handbook: Stages 3 – 5.*

What next?
Now go to page 74: **Comprehension.**

Unseen Text Assessment

Child: .... Age: .... Class: ....

Teacher: .... Date: ....

Comprehension

Finish reading the text with the child. Have a reading conversation to find out how well they understood what they read (some example questions are provided below). Circle the letter that best reflects their understanding.

KEY

C Complete
P Partial
N None
NE No evidence

Retells information in own words   AF2   Summarising   **C   P   N   NE**

Example: Where does this story take place?

At the beach.

Retells information   AF2   Summarising   **C   P   N   NE**

Example: Who saw some of the chest first?

Ben.

Makes inferences about characters' feelings   AF3   Imagining   **C   P   N   NE**

Example: How would you feel if you were there? Why?

Any sensible answer based on the text, *e.g. excited;* provides reasoning, *e.g. it might be very old.*

Makes inferences about events and information   AF3   Clarifying   **C   P   N   NE**

Example: Why did the children dig when all they saw was a point?

Any sensible answer based on the text, *e.g. they wanted to find out what it was.*

Makes appropriate predictions   AF3   Predicting   **C   P   N   NE**

Example: What do you think the children might do next?

Any sensible prediction based on the text, *e.g. show their parents.*

To see an example of a reading conversation, go to page 29
in **Assess & Progress** *Teacher's Handbook: Stages 3–5.*

Using the phonics checklists

The Blending and Segmenting Checklist and Grapheme-Phoneme
Checklist assess a child's basic phonics knowledge and their ability to
apply it. You can use them:

- at any time, to confirm a child's phonics knowledge and skills are at
  the level you expect
- when you notice errors in a child's use of phonics to read unfamiliar
  words, to find out just where the gaps or weaknesses lie
- when you notice that a child isn't using phonics as a reading strategy,
  to find out about their level of skill and knowledge.

The Blending and Segmenting Checklist includes example words
which can be replaced as required. You might want to make sure the
phonics content matches your teaching more exactly, or, if repeating
the checklist with a child, to use new words at an appropriate level
to ensure they haven't memorized the correct response rather
than used their phonics skills to work it out. An editable version of
the checklist can be found in the assessment resources area of the
Assess & Progress software.

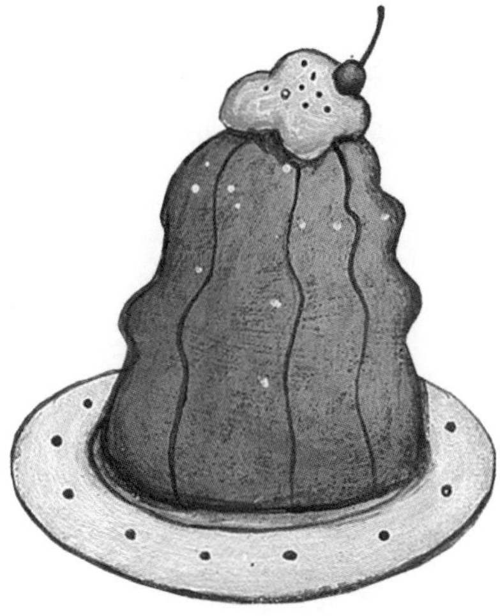

Blending and Segmenting Checklist

Name: .... Date: ....

Work through the tasks in order. For each task:
1. *Read the question and work through a practice example together.*
2. *Give the child a different example, and let them work through it as independently*
as possible, giving support if it's needed. Agree the answer.
3. *Repeat until you feel you can mark a result (✓ or ✗).*

Skill assessed	Questions, examples and suggested words	✓ / ✗
Can match letters to sounds (recognizes grapheme-phoneme correspondences)	Use the Grapheme-Phoneme Checklist on page 77 with flashcards showing the different graphemes to check the child's knowledge of which sounds are represented by which letters.	
Can hear rhymes in words	Do these words rhyme? Practice examples: cat fat (rhyme) cat pin (don't rhyme) What about: pie lie toe foot tin tick sing wing	
Can produce rhymes	Can you think of more words or nonsense words that rhyme? Practice example: pin rhymes with thin, bin, fin, lin, win … What about: cat wing	
Can hear the first sound in a word	Which sound do these words begin with? Practice examples: dog begins with d shop begins with sh What about: cap sun hen chip plug string	
Can hear the last sound in a word	Which sound do these words end with? Practice examples: dog ends with g tooth ends with th What about: log zip yes sun sing chimp	
Can hear the vowel sound in the middle of a word	Which vowel sound is in the middle of these words? Practice examples: a is in the middle of cat i is in the middle of pin What about: hen sun tap rain sheep road	

Can segment orally (say the sounds in a word)	Say the sounds in this word separately, showing a sound finger for each one. How many sounds are in the word?
	Practice example: For hen, we say h-e-n (3 sounds)
	What about: cat (3: c-a-t) wait (3: w-ai-t)
	                     sand (4: s-a-n-d) thick (3: th-i-ck)
	                     splash (5: s-p-l-a-sh)
	                     chimp (4: ch-i-m-p)	

Can blend orally (say sounds together to make a word)	What word am I sounding out? Practice example: g-o-t is got What about: k-i-t t-u-ck r-u-n f-i-zz m-o-th h-a-mm-er b-oo-s-t t-r-u-nk a-nn-oy Au-g-u-s-t	

Grapheme-Phoneme Checklist

Name: .... Date: ....

- Show the child flashcards one at a time, each one showing a different grapheme.
  Flashcards are provided on the assessment resources area of the Assess & Progress Software.
- Ask the child to say the sound each card represents.
- Mark their results (✓ or X) in the chart below.
- Note that the second column is a pronunciation guide, not part of the assessment.
- The checklist shows all 78 grapheme-phoneme correspondences required for children to reach reading fluency. Check children's ability to read them securely up to the grapheme-phonemes that they've been taught. Stop checking at the point that grapheme-phonemes haven't yet been taught.

Grapheme	As in	✓ / X
s	sat	
a	at	
t	tap	
p	pat	
i	in	
n	nap	
m	map	
d	dip	
g	gas	
o	on	
c	cat	
k	kid	
ck	kick	
e	pet	
u	dug	
r	rip	
h	hat	
b	bin	
f, ff	fit, puff	
l, ll	lip, doll	
ss	fuss	
j	jam	
v	van	
w	wet	
x	box	
y	yes	

Grapheme	As in	✓ / X
z, zz	zip, fizz	
qu	quack	
ch	chin	
sh	ship	
th	thick	
th	this	
ng	sing	
ai	pail	
ee	teeth	
igh	high	
oa	foal	
oo	hoot	
oo	shook	
ar	far	
or	fork	
ur	burn	
ow	owl	
oi	boil	
ear	hear	
air	pair	
ure	cure	
er	corner	
ay	say	
ou	out	
ie	lie	
ea	eat	

Grapheme	As in	✓ / X
oy	boy	
ir	girl	
ue	blue	
aw	saw	
wh	when	
ph	photo	
ew	new	
oe	toe	
au	Paul	
a-e	late	
e-e	even	
i-e	pile	
o-e	those	
u-e	tune	
i	kind	
o	old	
c	cent	
g	gem	
u	put	
ow	blow	
ie	field	
ea	bread	
er	her	
a	was	
y	by	
y	very	

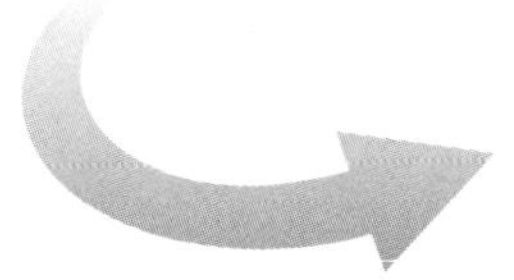

Problems and solutions

This section provides ideas for activities to use with children to strengthen the reading skills that assessment has revealed are weak. Use the list below to find suggestions for particular areas.

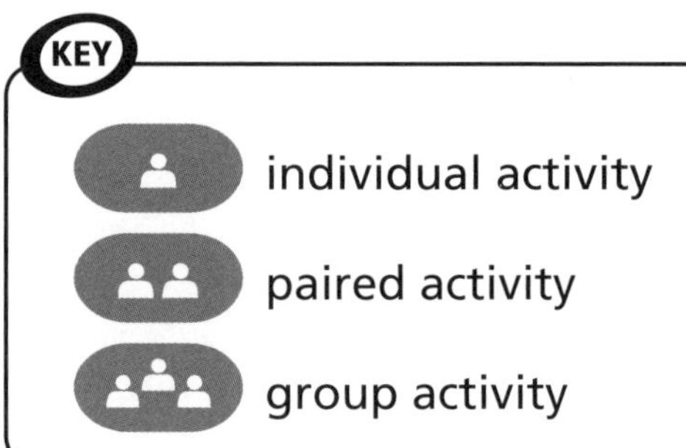

A Phonics knowledge and skills

1 Learning new sounds, letters or words
2 Segmenting orally
3 Blending to read
4 Blending orally
5 Grapheme recognition
6 Grapheme recognition – sounds represented by more than one letter
7 Grapheme recognition – unusual grapheme-phoneme correspondences
8 Identifying high frequency words (HFWs)
9 Reading learned, tricky high frequency words (HFWs)

B Other reading strategies

1 Confusing words that look similar
2 Substituting words that don't fit the context
3 Guessing words using context clues, e.g. pictures
4 Missing words out
5 Relying on one reading strategy
6 Using context, e.g. word order and grammar, to support reading

C Understanding a text

1 Recognizing mistakes
2 Making meaning

D Finding and recalling information

1 Recalling oral sequences
2 Recalling written sequences, retelling a story
3 Understanding the relationship between events in a story

E Inference and deduction

1 Interpreting a story and predicting events

F Understanding text structure and organization

1 Identifying simple text features

G Use of language

1 Vocabulary
2 Vocabulary – learning English for the first time
3 Recalling common patterns of language

H Preferences in reading

1 Commenting on preferences
2 Interest in reading

 Phonics knowledge and skills

1 Learning new sounds, letters or words

The child finds it difficult to learn new sounds, letters or words.

Use a multi-sensory approach to learning, combining visual, auditory and kinaesthetic methods.

Visual: Find an object in the room for the child to make a visual link to a sound or word; use different colours or different sizes of print to identify, e.g. the tricky bit in the word.

Auditory: Children hear you, another child or a recorded voice saying the sound or word.

Kinaesthetic: Let children associate the sound or word with movement, e.g. by shaping or handwriting the letters, or making a movement they can link to the sound, letter or word.

2 Segmenting orally

The child finds it difficult to say separately all the sounds in a word they hear.

You will need: *counters (4 or 5 for each child)*

Say a word, e.g. *cat*. Repeat it slowly, but without separating the sounds.

Ask children to say the word to themselves, and to think about how many different sounds there are in the word.

Ask them to say each sound out loud, and to push forward one counter for each sound. Agree the answer. If they struggle, model the answer, saying each sound then blending to say the whole word.

Step 1 Use 2- and 3-sound words, e.g. *in, up, as; sip, cup, dog*

Step 2 Use 2- and 3-sound words, e.g. *is, in, on; ship, this, rain, sheep*

Step 3 Use 3- and 4-sound words, e.g. *sad* and *sand, tip* and *trip, fog* and *frog, wet* and *went*; then *train, clean, smooth, paint*

Step 4 Use 2-, 3- and 4-sound words, e.g. *eat, out, owl; like, play, glue; clown, spray, plate.*

3 Blending to read

The child finds it difficult to identify the different sounds in a word they read.

You will need: *a magnetic whiteboard and letters, whiteboards and pens*

Show a word written with magnetic letters.

Ask children to separate the letters to show the separate sounds.

Next, ask them to copy the word onto their whiteboards and draw a sound button or line under each sound, then to blend the sounds to read the word.

Agree the answer. If they struggle, model the answer, saying each sound then blending to say the whole word.

Step 1	Use 2- and 3-sound words, e.g. *in, up, as; sip, cup, dog*
Step 2	Use 2- and 3-sound words, e.g. *is, in, on; ship, this, rain, sheep*
Step 3	Use 3- and 4-sound words, e.g. *sad* and *sand*, *tip* and *trip*, *fog* and *frog*, *wet* and *went*; then *train, clean, smooth, paint*
Step 4	Use 2-, 3- and 4-sound words, e.g. *eat, out, owl; like, play, glue; clown, spray, plate.*

4 Blending orally

The child finds it difficult to blend sounds they hear to say a word.

You will need: *an unbreakable tabletop mirror*

Ask the child to watch the shape of your mouth as you say the sounds in a word, e.g. *b-i-t.*

Ask them to say the same sounds, copying the shape of your mouth in a mirror. Repeat as needed, before asking them to blend to say the whole word.

Next, ask them to repeat the word, counting the sounds on sound fingers as they say them.

5 Grapheme recognition

The child finds it difficult to identify sounds from letters.

You will need: *magnetic whiteboards and letters*

Ask children to make a word with magnetic letters, e.g. *shop*, then to change one sound to make a different word, e.g. *ship.*

Discuss the new word they have made.

Ask them to change one more sound to make a different word, e.g. *chip.*

At first, say each new word you want them to make, e.g. change *shop* to *shock*, then *chock, chick, kick, kip, sip, ship, shop.*

Later, challenge children to make their own new words.

Step 1	Use simple 3-sound words, e.g. *cat, mat, map*
Step 2	Use 3-sound words, including some with sounds represented by more than one letter, e.g. *ran, rain, pain, pail, peel, pool*
Step 3	Use words with adjacent consonants, e.g. *clip, slip, slit, sleet, sleep*
Step 4	Focus on new phonemes, e.g. *bake, bike, pike, poke, pole, role, rule*

You will need: *pairs of cards showing the same two-letter sound, e.g.* ph, *or letters that represent the same sound, e.g.* ai *and* ay

Use the cards to play bingo, lotto, snap or pairs.

Ask children to look out for these groups of letters when they are reading. Remind them, if they stumble, that they have met the letters before in the game.

6 Grapheme recognition – sounds represented by more than one letter

The child finds it difficult to identify sounds represented by more than
one letter.

When reading an unfamiliar word, teach the child to:

1 Sound-talk words first, e.g. say the sounds _th-ere_.

2 Repeat, marking a sound button or line under each sound, e.g. _th ere_.

3 Blend the sounds to say the word.

7 Grapheme recognition – unusual grapheme-phoneme correspondences

The child finds it difficult to identify unusual letter-sound correspondences,
e.g. _ai_ in _said_.

During each reading session, make a note of any graphemes that are not
secure. Remind children to:

1 Sound out and blend the sounds in the word.

2 If it doesn't make sense, identify the tricky bit and think of other ways to
pronounce it.

3 Try other pronunciations until they read a word that makes sense.

4 Re-read the sentence to check that it does make sense.

5 If no pronunciation makes sense, ask for help.

You will need: _a copy of a text that includes examples of the problem letter
groups (graphemes)_
Tracking activity. Give the child a highlighter pen and ask them to highlight
their target letter groups in the text. For each target they find, ask the child to
say the sound, then the whole word. Support them to find all the target letter
groups in the text.

8 Identifying high frequency words (HFWs)

The child finds it difficult to identify high frequency words in texts.

During each reading session, make a note of high frequency words (HFWs) that
are not secure. Use them for activities like these:

You will need: _pairs of cards showing the same word, e.g._ can _or words that go
together, e.g. rhyming words like_ can _and_ van
Play bingo, lotto, snap or pairs.
Ask children to look out for these words when they are reading. Remind
them, if they stumble over one of the words, that they have met it before in
the game.

You will need: *a copy of a text that includes problem HFWs*

Tracking activity. Give the child a highlighter pen and ask them to track down their target words. For each target they find, ask them to read the word aloud. Support them to find all the target words in the text.

You will need: *a poster showing a wall with ten bricks in it, blank cards to be stuck onto the wall as bricks*

Give children ten blank cards that match the bricks in a 'word wall' poster. Ask them to copy ten words you want them to learn onto their 'bricks'. Give them opportunities to find and use the words in different contexts, e.g. word games, flashcards, and reading, speaking and writing activities. Each time a child recognizes a word, mark a tick on their brick. When there are five ticks, ask the child to stick the brick onto their word wall. Plan a reward for when the wall is built.

9 Reading learned, tricky high frequency words (HFWs)

The child finds it difficult to identify and read tricky (irregular, non-decodable) high frequency words (HFWs) they have learned.

Find out more.

1 Check whether the child has had a vision test recently, and if so what the results were. If not, suggest they have one.

2 Play a game to assess visual memory. Put three objects on a tray, and ask the child to try to remember what they are.

Ask the child to look away while you remove one object and rearrange the others. Can the child say which object has gone? Alternatively, ask the child to look away and list all the objects on the tray.

Once the child is correct twice in a row, increase the number of objects by one and repeat.

You will need: *flashcards in pairs, showing graphemes, words, or words and pictures*

Play pairs. Children lay the cards out face-down and take turns to pick up two cards. If they match, they keep the two cards. The player with the most pairs at the end wins.

You will need: *two or three pictures of varying complexity*

Show the child a simple picture. Let them look at it for ten seconds, then cover it and ask questions. Gradually increase the complexity of the picture and the time given to look at it.

You will need: *a simple poem or rhyme*

Give children a poem or rhyme to learn, including, e.g. line breaks and punctuation. Ask them to write it out from memory as accurately as they can.

Teach tricky high frequency words, emphasizing the known and 'tricky' bits, so that children learn to read these words on sight. When children meet a new irregular word, support them in working out the known and 'tricky' bits in it. Encourage them to use phonics to read as much as they can of the word.

Encourage the child to build a wide vocabulary – see the suggestions in section G.

Compare the child's visual and auditory memories. A significantly better visual memory than auditory memory is often associated with dyslexia. If a child seems to have this or other problems with short-term memory, refer them to the special needs teacher.

B Other reading strategies

1 Confusing words that look similar

The child confuses words that look similar, e.g. *on* and *one*, *of* and *for*.

Support the child by:
- reminding them to look at individual words, and to slow down if they're reading too fast
- encouraging them to sound out and blend each problem word
- asking questions to encourage them to check meaning, e.g. *Does that last sentence make sense?*

If errors match the child's dialect, e.g. *we were* becomes *we was*, they are making sense of the text even though they're not reading accurately. Revisit the word once the child's read to the end of the sentence, so as not to interrupt the flow.

2 Substituting words that don't fit the context

The child substitutes words that don't fit the context, e.g. *We were to the seaside*, or has difficulty recalling common patterns of language.

You will need: *text to read aloud containing patterned language*
Oral cloze. When you're reading aloud, ask children to fill in the missing words when you pause. Use familiar patterned language from traditional tales, e.g. *once upon a _____ ; run, run as fast as ___ ___ ;* or use repeated words or phrases from books the children know well.

You will need: *tabs of peel-off sticky paper*
Written cloze. Select an unfamiliar book well within the child's reading level. Cover key words. Can the child predict what the words might be?

You will need: *whiteboards and pens*

Show a word the children can decode, from which a grapheme is missing. Ask them to write what the word might be, e.g. _ot could be *pot*, *hot*, *cot*, etc. Next, show the incomplete word in a sentence, e.g. *It was very _ot that day.* Agree what the word is most likely to be. Discuss how they know, e.g. the word has to be an adjective.

3 Guessing words using context clues, e.g. pictures

You will need: *phonics checklists (pages 75–77)*

Use the Blending and Segmenting and Grapheme-Phoneme Checklists to identify any gaps in phonics skills or knowledge. Return to texts at an appropriate level. Support children in approaching unfamiliar words by using phonics as their first strategy.

4 Missing words out

The child misses words, reads them inaudibly or waits to be told what they are.

The text may be too challenging. Try an easier text, e.g. a book at the previous Oxford Reading Tree stage or Book Band. To build confidence, gently encourage the child to have a go at the problem words. Emphasize the need to make meaning.

5 Relying on one reading strategy

The child mostly relies on one reading strategy, and reading accuracy or comprehension is limited.

Find out more about the child's skill level in different reading strategies, to pinpoint areas for practice. Use a miscue analysis (Step 2 of a Reading Assessment), Unseen Text card or the phonics checklists to help you (see pages 65–77 for more detail on how to do this).

6 Using context, e.g. word order and grammar, to support reading

The child has difficulty making meaning, makes mistakes in reading without pausing or self-correcting, is unaware of word order or grammar.

You will need: *interactive whiteboard or paper, pen and scissors, a simple sentence that can be rearranged*

1 Write a simple sentence, e.g. *The dog bit the cat.* Ask the child to read it, cut it into words and remake the sentence.

2 Ask them to rearrange the words to make a different sentence, e.g. *The cat bit the dog.* Discuss how the meaning changes.

3 Provide one or two adjectives and discuss the different places they could go in the sentence, e.g. *The little cat bit the big dog.* Discuss how the meaning changes.

4 Ask the child to identify any words that could be replaced by 'better' words. Talk about what 'better' means. Discuss which words could be replaced and the effect on the sentence, e.g. *The tiny cat ate the huge dog.*

5 You could follow this activity with a written cloze activity. Cover words in an appropriate text, and ask the child to predict what they might be. Discuss the reasons for their choices.

C Understanding a text

1 Recognizing mistakes

The child doesn't pause, re-read or self-correct, or recognize mistakes.

Encourage children to self-check regularly. For example, ask questions to check:
- Meaning, e.g. *Can you explain that last bit to me?*
- Reading accuracy, e.g. *Did all the words in that sentence sound right to you?*
- Fluency and expression, e.g. *Where should you pause on that page? How do you think someone would say that in real life?*

Ask these kinds of questions when the child has read correctly, as well as incorrectly, and encourage them to re-read. When they pause, re-read or self-correct, give praise.

Support the child in developing strategies for self-correction:

1 Using phonics skills first: sounding out, identifying tricky bits and thinking of 'soundalike' words.

2 Re-reading and reading around the word to see if any of the soundalike words fit with the grammar and meaning.

3 Checking against other context clues, such as pictures and overall storyline.

2 Making meaning

The child decodes accurately, but has difficulty making meaning.

You will need: *simple pictures, jumbled captions*
Ask children to read captions and match them to pictures.

You will need: *simple captions*
Ask children to draw a picture to match each caption.

You will need: *text for 3–4 pages of a book*
Ask children to make a simple book, drawing pictures to go with it.
If appropriate, challenge children to continue the text for one or two more pages.

D Finding and recalling information

1 Recalling oral sequences

The child finds it difficult to remember sequences they've heard, e.g. a set of instructions given orally.

Find out more:

1 Check whether the child has had a hearing test recently, and if so what the results were. If they haven't had one, or the results are in doubt, suggest they have one.
2 Check the child's memory of what they hear. Can they remember: the first sound in a 3- or 4-phoneme word; the beginning of a 5- or 6-word sentence; the first instruction in a sequence of three?

> If children seem to have problems with short-term memory, refer them to the special needs teacher, who may choose to use a diagnostic memory test.

Play aural memory games. For example, each child takes a turn to say "I went shopping and I bought …", remembering the items and adding a new one each time. This reinforces memory and encourages strategies for remembering.

Learn short poems and rhymes as a class. Practise reciting these as performance poetry, with gestures and intonation.

2 Recalling written sequences, retelling a story

The child finds it difficult to remember sequences, to put pictures in order, to retell events in a story in the correct order.

Find out more. Ask children to recite some sequences they have been taught, e.g. their own name and address, songs or rhymes, the alphabet, days of the week, months of the year.

You will need: *interactive whiteboard, counting equipment*
Make repeating sequences for children to remember and continue, e.g. coloured beads repeating: red blue white, red blue white … ; names of animals repeating: horse cow goat, horse cow goat … .
For extra challenge, increase the number of elements to make repeating sequences of 4 or 5, or change the sequence in a predictable way and ask children to continue it, e.g. red blue white, white red blue, blue white red, red blue white … .

You will need: *digital camera and printer*
Photograph children as they make something, e.g. while cooking. Ask children to select five photos, and put them in the right order to show what happened.

You will need: *digital camera and printer*
Photograph children re-enacting a story through role play, or with puppets or toys. Ask children to select and sequence some of the pictures, then to retell the story.

You will need: *laminated pictures cut from old reading books*
Ask children to sequence some of the pictures and tell the story to go with them. This is a very powerful way to encourage children to engage with stories and books.

> If children seem to be having problems with this, consider consulting the special needs teacher. Children with dyslexia often struggle to remember sequences.

3 Understanding the relationship between events in a story
The child finds it difficult to identify the beginning, middle and end of a story, or to understand how or why events in a story follow each other.

You will need: *a blank storyboard (Activity Master 1 on page 100)*
Make a storyboard. Together, discuss the events in a familiar story. Explain to children that they are going to draw the story as a storyboard (a series of pictures like the frames of a cartoon strip) showing the main events. Begin by asking which events they would show if they could only show three, so that they have to decide on the three most important. Explain that they can draw more events, but must include these three.

E Inference and deduction

1 Interpreting a story and predicting events
The child finds it difficult to predict what might happen in a story or come up with alternative events; to engage imaginatively with the story or characters; or to deduce, infer or interpret information from texts.

You will need: *a picture you think is likely to interest the child*
Find out more. Have a conversation with the child about an interesting picture, asking questions on three levels:
- **What's in it?** – questions about what the picture explicitly shows.
- **Can you work it out?** – questions which can be answered using clues in the

picture (deduction), e.g. if the picture shows someone yawning, ask, *What time of day do you think it is?*

● **What do you think?** – questions which ask the child to empathize with the characters in the picture and suggest answers based on what they think (inference). Prompt the child to explain their answer, e.g. *Do you think she's the little boy's mother? Why?*

If the child can answer comprehension questions about a picture at these three different levels (**What's in it? Can you work it out? What do you think?**), it may be that they need to be taught that text carries meaning, and encouraged as a reader to make meaning. Go on to ask the same kinds of questions about texts you read aloud to the child, and about texts they read to you.

Ask questions to encourage children to expand on events and characters in stories, and to build a world around the characters in the books they read.

You will need: *a character web (Activity Master 2 on page 101)*
Ask the child to draw a picture of a character, and add words that describe the character. Encourage them to add as many as they can think of.

Children recreate an event or scene from a book by role-playing. For extra challenge, ask them to come up with a scene not in the book, e.g. an alternative ending, or something happened but wasn't described. Prompt them by discussing the plot and characters.

You will need: *a copy of the start of a story, puppets or toys*
Ask children to read the beginning of a story together, and to recreate it with puppets or toys representing the characters. Ask them to decide what might happen next, and to use the characters to create the scene.

You will need: *simple props*
Ask children, in pairs, to read a story or part of a story. Present the group with a selection of suitable props, briefly describing each one. Pairs should choose a prop to go with a character from the story, then prepare an explanation about why their prop suits the character. This might involve playing the character. Ask pairs to present to the group, explaining their choice of prop.

> If the child can't answer the questions and they may have general cognitive difficulties, you may want to consult your special needs teacher.
>
> If they can answer the questions but their comprehension of texts they read seems much poorer, consider consulting with the special needs teacher – you'd expect dyslexic children's responses to questions based on pictures and heard stories to be better than their response to questions based on texts they have read.

F Understanding text structure and organization

1 Identifying simple text features

The child is unaware of different text features, or finds it difficult to identify different parts of a text.

You will need: *a copy of a text cut into parts, e.g. a short story cut into beginning, middle and end, a set of instructions*
Ask children to put the text in the correct order. Agree the answer and discuss how they reached it.

You will need: *a page of a non-fiction book cut into its different features, e.g. pictures, labels, titles, main text*
Ask children to design a page of a non-fiction text from its individual parts.

G Use of language

1 Vocabulary

The child has limited vocabulary.

Play *The Caretaker's Cat*. Players take it in turns to complete the sentence *The caretaker's cat eats …*, adding a new item each time. Each new item should begin with the next letter in the alphabet, e.g. the first player might say *The caretaker's cat eats apples*, the second *The caretaker's cat eats apples and biscuits*, and so on.
Alternatively, use the sentence *The caretaker's cat is a … cat* to ask children to find adjectives.

Play Animal Alliteration. Players take it in turns to work through the alphabet, e.g. *The ant was angry, The bat was blue*, etc. Encourage children to use more than one adjective if they can, the more inventive the better.

2 Vocabulary – learning English for the first time

The child is learning English for the first time, and has limited vocabulary.

Invite the child to share one or two of their favourite storybooks with you. Ask them to tell you about the pictures. During the conversation, make sure most of the objects in the picture are named. Discuss the colours, characters, feelings and actions illustrated, as appropriate.

3 Recalling common patterns of language

The child finds it difficult to read common patterns of language accurately, makes similar mistakes with repeated language.

See activities in section B.

H Preferences in reading

1 Commenting on preferences

The child shows few preferences in reading, or doesn't comment on preferences.

You will need: *a familiar book*
Explore a familiar book with the child, discussing which bits they like or dislike. Do they like stories or learning new things when they read? Are there particular characters they enjoy reading about? How do they like to feel when they read a book – scared, worried, giggly, excited?

You will need: *a blank reading journal page (Activity Master 3 on page 102)*
Make a class reading journal to record responses to a text. Include things like personal responses, character studies, diary entries, predictions, further investigations about the setting, discussions about the events, storyboards, etc.

2 Interest in reading

The child isn't very interested in reading.

You will need: *prepared quiz questions*
Set book quizzes. Once enough children have read a book (whether individually or in groups), create a book quiz for them. It can be as simple or as elaborate as you like. Allow children to have copies of the book to look at as you ask the questions. The quiz format could be individual, pair, or team, with answers given in turns, by 'first hand up' or written down. Questions can be of a variety of types (the examples given here are based on the Stage 5 Biff, Chip and Kipper story, *The New Baby*):

Who am I? e.g. *My wife is going to have a baby. Who am I?*
What did they say? e.g. *What did Wilma's Mum say when the wheel came off the buggy?*
Why do you think …? e.g. *Why did Wilma's Mum give the old buggy to Jo?*
Can you see …? e.g. *How many pairs of glasses are there on pages 2–3?*
What happened after …? e.g. *What happened after Jo asked Kipper to change the baby's nappy?*

Reassessing children

Once you have worked with a child on weak areas and you're considering whether they are ready to move on, you can either:

- use the evidence you've already gathered to decide whether they're ready to move on – this might include their Reading Progress Checklist, the Guided Reading Record, their work from Problems and solutions activities and any other information collected by continuous assessment

OR

- reassess, using a new Reading Assessment to confirm they're ready to read at a new stage.

If you decide to carry out another Reading Assessment, you can use:

- another *Assess & Progress* Benchmark Book at the appropriate stage (go to page 38)
- the Unseen Text card from the appropriate stage, if you haven't yet used it (go to page 68)
- a Reading Assessment of your own, using an unread book at an appropriate level.

Preparing your own Reading Assessment

- Choose a suitable book at the right level.
- Use the editable Blank Reading Assessment in the assessment resources area of the *Assess & Progress* software.
- Choose a section of text of about 100 words to use for the miscue analysis. The section should be fairly close to the beginning of the book, but far enough in for the child to have settled into the session. (Remember you don't have to finish reading the book during a Reading Assessment.)
- Plan some comprehension questions to ask. Use the questions from the *Assess & Progress* Reading Assessments at the same stage as a guide. Make sure your questions give reasonable coverage of expected reading behaviours for this stage by checking against the Assessment Focuses in the Guided Reading Record.

If this Reading Assessment shows that the child isn't ready to move on, try to identify specific barriers to progress. Continue with additional reading opportunities at the same level, as well as making sure they get more practice in their target areas. Talk to your special needs teacher to see if the child needs more specialist assessment or intervention.

Guided Reading Record Level 1

Group: .... Date: ....

Oxford Reading Tree

ASSESS & PROGRESS

For ideas on how to use this record, go to page 31 in Assess & Progress Teacher's Handbook: Stages 3–5.

AF1 use a range of strategies, including accurate decoding of text, to read for meaning	AF2 understand, describe, select or retrieve information, events or ideas from text and use quotation and reference to text	AF3 deduce, infer or interpret information, events or ideas from texts	AF4 identify and comment on the structure and organisation of texts, including grammatical and presentational features	AF5 explain and comment on writers' use of language, including grammatical and literary features at word and sentence level	AF6 identify and comment on writers' purposes and viewpoints, and the overall effect of the text on the reader	AF7 relate texts to their social, cultural and historical traditions
some high frequency words read on sight ↑ 100 high frequency words ↑ 75–100 high frequency words including 30 tricky ↑ 75 high frequency words **some unfamiliar words decoded using phonic strategies** ↑ sounds out unfamiliar words, usually accurately, some awareness of alternative pronunciations of graphemes ↑ often sounds out simple words accurately, also attempts to read words with adjacent consonants ↑ attempts common and simple decodable words **some use of punctuation** ↑ takes account of full stops, and some other punctuation, e.g. commas ↑ usually pauses at full stops ↑ sometimes pauses at full stops	**recalls simple points from familiar texts** ↑ retells a story by picking out some significant events ↑ recalls some key events in a story ↑ names some characters in a known story, or known characters in a new story **picks out some pages of interest, *e.g. pictures, characters, events*** ↑ often clear where to look for information in a familiar book, e.g. about characters in a story or facts in a non-fiction book ↑ searches through a familiar book to find basic information, using text or pictures ↑ uses text or pictures to select some favourite pages in a familiar book	**makes reasonable, simple inferences, *e.g. who is speaking*** ↑ simple inferences about a familiar text, e.g. which dinosaurs are most frightening ↑ makes simple inferences, often from pictures, e.g. who is speaking ↑ with support, makes some simple inferences **comments on or asks questions about meaning of, *e.g. illustrations, beginning of text*** ↑ in a familiar text, can sometimes point to evidence in words or pictures to explain comments ↑ e.g. an event, illustrations, information on more than one page of a non-fiction book ↑ e.g. an event, illustrations, information in a non-fiction book	**some understanding of simple text features** ↑ can identify a range of features, e.g. titles and headings, different fonts, captions, labels, contents page, blurb ↑ can identify ways of creating emphasis, e.g. capitals, large or bold print ↑ can identify most obvious features, e.g. headings and titles	**comments on obvious, simple aspects of language, *e.g. rhymes and refrains, significant words and phrases like "Oh no!"*** ↑ with support, can pick out descriptive words, e.g. scruffy ↑ comments on significant words and phrases ↑ able to spot rhymes and repeating phrases within a text	**expresses simple preferences, often linked to own experience** ↑ with support, sometimes gives further reasons for liking or disliking a book, character or event ↑ some comments about likes and dislikes, often linked to own experience ↑ returns to favourite books independently	**distinguishes between simple features of well-known story and information texts, *e.g. goodies and baddies, photos and drawings*** ↑ talks about unfamiliar books making reference to familiar features ↑ talks about features of known books, *e.g. good and bad characters, photos and drawings* ↑ with support, begins to distinguish between texts and their uses, e.g. story, information, instructions

Notes:

Guided Reading Record Level 2

Group: ....   Date: ....

For ideas on how to use this record, go to page 31 in Assess & Progress Teacher's Handbook: Stages 3–5.

AF1 use a range of strategies, including accurate decoding of text, to read for meaning	AF2 understand, describe, select or retrieve information, events or ideas from text and use quotation and reference to text	AF3 deduce, infer or interpret information, events or ideas from texts	AF4 identify and comment on the structure and organisation of texts, including grammatical and presentational features at text level	AF5 explain and comment on writers' use of language, including grammatical and literary features at word and sentence level	AF6 identify and comment on writers' purposes and viewpoints, and the overall effect of the text on the reader	AF7 relate texts to their social, cultural and historical traditions
range of key words read on sight 100 high frequency words, plus ↑ about a further 200 common words ↑ about a further 130 common words ↑ about a further 70 common words	**some specific, straightforward information recalled, *e.g. names of characters, main ingredients*** ↑ sometimes draws together information from different places in the text ↑ recalls significant events, characters and settings in stories ↑ answers simple questions by recalling main ideas	**simple, plausible inference about events and information, using evidence from text, *e.g. how a character is feeling, what makes a plant grow*** ↑ with support, suggests extensions, e.g. alternative endings for a story ↑ sometimes gives reasons why things happen or characters change ↑ shows basic understanding of main ideas and characters, e.g. by making reasonable predictions	**some awareness of use of features of organisation, *e.g. beginning and ending of story, types of punctuation*** ↑ when asked, can identify a few basic features of organisation, e.g. recognises alphabetical order ↑ can use features of information texts, e.g. contents page, index, and beginning as well as end ↑ knows what has happened at the beginning and end of a story	**some effective language choices noted, *e.g. 'slimy' is a good word there*** ↑ can sometimes identify appropriate alternative words ↑ sometimes identifies effective word choices ↑ with support, shows some awareness that authors select words	**some awareness that writers have viewpoints and purposes, *e.g. 'it tells you how to do something', 'she thinks it's not fair'*** ↑ with support, makes basic comments on writer's purpose in story, e.g. "She makes it scary" ↑ often identifies writer's purpose, especially for non-fiction, e.g. "It's about how frogs grow" ↑ knows that stories and non-fiction books have different purposes	**general features of a few text types identified, *e.g. information books, stories, print media*** ↑ some basic similarities between texts identified, e.g. they both have goodies and baddies / tell you about dinosaurs / have photos ↑ general features of a few non-fiction text types identified, e.g. letters, invitations, instructions, reports and recounts ↑ identifies different text types from a selection
unfamiliar words decoded using appropriate strategies, *e.g. blending sounds* ↑ mostly decodes silently and independently ↑ mostly decodes silently, sometimes needs support ↑ decodes some words out loud, with some errors ↑ self-corrects independently ↑ sometimes self-corrects independently ↑ self-corrects with support	**generally clear idea of where to look for information, *e.g. about characters, topics*** ↑ sometimes uses features, e.g. contents page or index, to find information ↑ identifies where information needed to answer a simple question can be found ↑ uses headings and pictures to identify where in a book to find information	**comments based on textual cues, sometimes misunderstood** ↑ responses to text are generally based on imagined own feelings, rather than what a character is feeling ↑ comments based on words as well as pictures and are often appropriate ↑ sometimes able to refer to words as well as pictures when commenting		**some familiar patterns of language identified, *e.g. once upon a time, first, next, last*** ↑ can retell a simple story making some use of original language patterns ↑ begins to link language patterns with text types, e.g. numbering with instructions, 'once upon a time' with traditional stories ↑ finishes familiar language patterns e.g. "Once upon …", "Happily ever …"		**some awareness that books are set in different times and places** ↑ sometimes finds evidence for setting ↑ with support, finds evidence for setting ↑ often identifies setting, but may not be able to explain how they know
some fluency and expression, *e.g. taking account of speech marks* ↑ reads with fluency and some expression ↑ reads with fluency, adds expression with support ↑ reads familiar texts with some fluency, usually using punctuation					**simple statements about likes and dislikes in reading, sometimes with reasons** ↑ with support, expresses simple personal response, e.g. "It was funny when Dad dropped the jelly" ↑ chooses own reading, makes simple comments ↑ chooses personal reading, sometimes giving simple reasons	
developing reading stamina ↑ reads some unfamiliar texts independently ↑ reads a few pages of unfamiliar texts independently ↑ reads familiar texts independently	**Notes:**					

Reading Progress Checklist Level 1

Group: .... Date: ....

Use this chart to record progress during the year.

Write the date you first observe a behaviour. Add ticks on at least two further occasions when the behaviour is noted.

Date	Level 1		Date	Level 1		Date	Level 1
AF1	reads 75 high frequency words on sight	→		reads 75–100 high frequency words on sight, including 30 tricky words	→		reads 100 high frequency words on sight
	attempts common and simple decodable words	→		often sounds out simple words accurately, also attempts to read words with adjacent consonants	→		sounds out unfamiliar words, usually accurately, some awareness of alternative pronunciations of graphemes
	sometimes pauses at full stops	→		usually pauses at full stops	→		takes account of full stops, and some other punctuation, e.g. commas
AF2	names some characters in a known story, or known characters in a new story	→		recalls some key events in a story	→		retells a story by picking out some significant events
	uses text or pictures to select some favourite pages in a familiar book	→		searches through a familiar book to find basic information, using text or pictures	→		often clear where to look for information in a familiar book, e.g. about characters in a story or facts in a non-fiction book
AF3	with support, makes some simple inferences	→		makes simple inferences, often from pictures, e.g. who is speaking	→		simple inferences about a familiar text, e.g. which dinosaurs are most frightening
	comments on or asks about an event, illustrations, information in a non-fiction book	→		comments on or asks about an event, illustrations, information on more than one page of a non-fiction book	→		in a familiar text, can sometimes point to evidence in words or pictures to explain comments
AF4	can identify most obvious features, e.g. headings and titles	→		can identify ways of creating emphasis, e.g. capitals, large or bold print	→		can identify a range of features, e.g. titles and headings, different fonts, captions, labels, contents page, blurb
AF5	able to spot rhymes and repeating phrases within a text	→		comments on significant words and phrases	→		with support, can pick out descriptive words, e.g. scruffy
AF6	returns to favourite books independently	→		some comments about likes and dislikes, often linked to own experience	→		with support, sometimes gives further reasons for liking or disliking a book, character or event
AF7	with support, begins to distinguish between texts and their uses, e.g. story, information, instructions	→		talks about features of known books, e.g. good and bad characters, photos and drawings	→		talks about unfamiliar books making reference to familiar features

Reading Progress Checklist Level 1–2

Group: .... Date: ....

Use this chart to record progress during the year.

Write the date you first observe a behaviour. Add ticks on at least two further occasions when the behaviour is noted.

	Date	Level 1		Date	Level 1		Date	Level 2	
AF1		reads 75–100 high frequency words on sight, including 30 tricky	→		reads 100 high frequency words on sight			reads 100 high frequency words, plus about a further 70 common words on sight	→
		often sounds out simple words accurately, also attempts to read words with adjacent consonants	→		sounds out unfamiliar words, usually accurately, some awareness of alternative pronunciations of graphemes		→	decodes some words out loud, with some errors	→
								self-corrects with support	→
		usually pauses at full stops	→		takes account of full stops, and some other punctuation, e.g. commas			reads familiar texts with some fluency, usually using punctuation	→
								reads familiar texts independently	→
AF2		recalls some key events in a story	→		retells a story by picking out some significant events			answers simple questions by recalling main ideas	→
							→	uses headings and pictures to identify where in a book to find information	→
		searches through a familiar book to find basic information, using text or pictures	→		often clear where to look for information in a familiar book, e.g. about characters in a story or facts in a non-fiction book				
AF3		makes simple inferences, often from pictures, e.g. who is speaking	→		simple inferences about a familiar text, e.g. which dinosaurs are most frightening			shows basic understanding of main ideas and characters, e.g. by making reasonable predictions	→
							→		
		comments on or asks about an event, illustrations, information on more than one page of a non-fiction book	→		in a familiar text, can sometimes point to evidence in words or pictures to explain comments			sometimes able to refer to words as well as pictures when commenting	→
AF4		can identify ways of creating emphasis, e.g. capitals, large or bold print	→		can identify a range of features, e.g. titles and headings, different fonts, captions, labels, contents page, blurb		→	knows what has happened at the beginning and end of a story	→
AF5		comments on significant words and phrases	→		with support, can pick out descriptive words, e.g. scruffy			with support, shows some awareness that authors can select from different words finishes	→
							→	familiar language patterns, e.g. "Once upon …", "Happily ever …"	→
AF6		some comments about likes and dislikes, often linked to own experience	→		with support, sometimes gives further reasons for liking or disliking a book, character or event			knows that stories and non-fiction books have different purposes	→
							→	chooses personal reading, sometimes giving simple reasons	→
AF7		talks about features of known books, e.g. good and bad characters, photos and drawings	→		talks about unfamiliar books making reference to familiar features			can identify different text types from a selection	→
							→	often identifies when or where a story is set, but may not be able to explain how they know	→

Reading Assessment Class Tracking Chart

Group: .... Date: ......

Use this chart to summarize the results of your class's Benchmark Book Reading Assessments.

Name	Date	Curriculum level	Oxford Reading Tree Stage / Book Band	Notes

Class Reading Progress Chart

Group: .... Date: ....

Use this chart to record your class's progress during the year.

When you assess children, write their names or initials in the appropriate space.

The shaded areas show you average attainment for reading in Year 1.

	Early Learning Goals			National Curriculum Level					
	working towards / within	working securely within	working beyond	1C	1B	1A	2C	2B	2A
Year 1 Autumn term									
Year 1 Spring term									
Year 1 Summer term									

Certificate for Reading

This certificate goes to

for

Good work!

from

____

Certificate for Reading

This certificate goes to

for

Good work!
from

____

AM
1

Name ....

ASSESS & PROGRESS

A Storyboard

Draw your story in the boxes. Write the title: ....

AM 2

Oxford Reading Tree

ASSESS & PROGRESS

A Character Web

Draw your character in the box.

Write some labels to describe your character.

Name ....

Book Review

Book title ....

Author ....

Date ....

Did you like the book? ☐ 👍 ☐ ✋ ☐ 👎

My drawing about this book:

The character I like best is ....

....

Name ....

Come to the Jumble Sale!

Where: ....

When: ....

Oxford Reading Tree
ASSESS & PROGRESS

Name ....

This certificate goes to

....

for ....

....

Well done!

Name ....

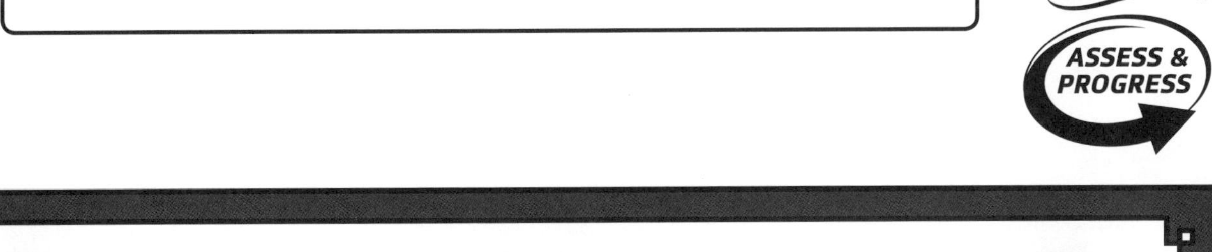

Come to my Party!

Please come to ....

....

On ....

At ....

From ....

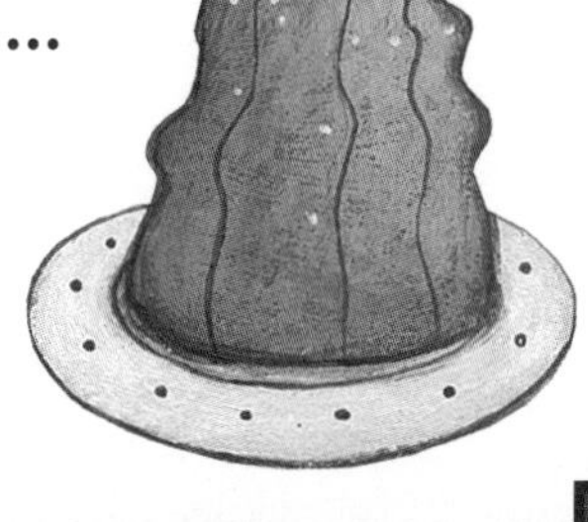

Notes

Notes

Notes

Notes

Notes

Notes

More teaching support from Oxford Reading Tree

Oxford Reading Tree offers a wide range of Primary classroom resources for fun, focused practice of reading and literacy skills. Find out more at **www.oup.com/oxed/primary/literacy/ort**

Oxford Reading Tree Magic Page software

Bring your favourite Biff, Chip and Kipper stories to life – talk, read, edit and explore.

Meet the author and illustrator! Magic Page features Roderick Hunt and Alex Brychta talking about each story.

For more information and how to order, go to our website at **www.oup.com/oxed/primary/literacy/ort**

Sequencing Cards Photocopy Masters

For Stages 1–4

ISBN 978 019 918473 6

Extended Stories Photocopy Masters

For Stages 1–4

ISBN 978 0 19 918474 3

Group Activity Sheets

Stages 1–3   ISBN 978 0 19 918472 9

Stages 4–5   ISBN 978 0 19 918960 1

Stages 6–9   ISBN 978 0 19 918961 8

Context cards

Set of 100 words

ISBN 978 0 19 916138 6

Oxford Reading Tree Dictionary

Hardback   ISBN 978 0 19 911638 6

Big Book   ISBN 978 0 19 911640 9

Story CDs for Stages 1–7

Your pupils will delight in listening to their favourite stories – perfect for developing speaking and listening skills.

Stages 1 and 1+   ISBN 978 0 19 846645 1

Stage 2   ISBN 978 0 19 846646 8

Stage 3   ISBN 978 0 19 846647 5

Stage 4   ISBN 978 0 19 846648 2

Stage 5   ISBN 978 0 19 846649 9

Stages 6 and 7   ISBN 978 0 19 846650 5

Achievement Stickers pack

ISBN 978 0 19 918951 9

Song Book and CD

Ideal for Letters and Sounds Phase 1

ISBN 978 0 19 321369 2

Floppy Hand Puppet

ISBN 978 0 19 845647 6

Finger Puppets

Pack A – Biff, Chip, Kipper, Floppy, Mum and Dad

ISBN 978 0 19 919304 2

Pack B – Gran, Mrs May, Anneena, Nadim, Wilf and Wilma

ISBN 978 0 19 919305 9

Oxford Reading Tree Games

Games Stages 1–3

The pack contains:
A large board, three double-sided small boards, twelve lotto boards for playing key word lotto, 74 character cards, 74 key words and character tiles, character jigsaws, counters, dice, photocopiable simple instruction leaflet.

ISBN 978 0 19 916450 9

Games Stages 4–5

The pack contains:
A large, double-sided board, 2 lotto boards (double-sided) – four each for Stage 4 and Stage 5; 4 small boards, 29 clue cards, 26 word tiles, 48 picture cards, 34 sentence cards, 48 lotto word tiles for each set, 66 letter tiles, 8 character tiles, Magic Key tile, blank cards and tiles in case of losses, sample Achievement sticker.

ISBN 978 0 19 918944 1

Games Stages 6–9

The pack contains:
1 double-sided board with 96 letter tiles (48 each game), 3 small double-sided boards with 48 letter tiles, 44 word tiles and 24 sentence cards, 2 sets of card games with 24 sentence cards, plus Teaching Notes with photocopiable material included.

ISBN 978 0 19 919252 6